EVER

GUIDE TO POTTY TRAINING

Dear Reader,

Congratulations! If you are reading this book, you probably have a son or daughter and are getting ready to begin potty training. As you read these chapters, it is important to remember that every child is different and no one method is perfect for every child. For this reason, there are multiple methods outlined as well as multiple signs identified to help you tailor your potty-training program to fit your child. If you try one program and see your child struggling, do not give up! There are always more ways to teach your child to use the potty, and it may just be that your child is not quite ready yet. Whatever the reason, this book will help you learn more about what to look for, what to teach, and how to help your child ease into a diaper-free world.

Kim Bookout
and Karen Williams

The EVERYTHING Series

These handy, accessible books give you all you need to tackle a difficult project, gain a new hobby, or even brush up on something you learned back in school but have since forgotten. You can read from cover to cover or just pick out information from our four useful boxes.

 Alerts: Urgent warnings

 Essentials: Quick handy tips

 Facts: Important snippets of information

 Questions: Answers to common questions

When you're done reading, you can finally say you know **EVERYTHING®**!

PUBLISHER Karen Cooper

DIRECTOR OF ACQUISITIONS AND INNOVATION Paula Munier

MANAGING EDITOR, EVERYTHING® SERIES Lisa Laing

COPY CHIEF Casey Ebert

ACQUISITIONS EDITOR Brett Palana-Shanahan

SENIOR DEVELOPMENT EDITOR Brett Palana-Shanahan

EDITORIAL ASSISTANT Ross Weisman

EVERYTHING® SERIES COVER DESIGNER Erin Alexander

LAYOUT DESIGNERS Colleen Cunningham, Elisabeth Lariviere, Ashley Vierra, Denise Wallace

Visit the entire Everything® series at *www.everything.com*

THE
EVERYTHING®
GUIDE TO
POTTY
TRAINING

A practical guide to finding the best
approach for you and your child

Kim Bookout, DNP, RN, CPNP and Karen Williams

Avon, Massachusetts

Copyright © 2010 by F+W Media, Inc.
All rights reserved.
This book, or parts thereof, may not be reproduced in any
form without permission from the publisher; exceptions are
made for brief excerpts used in published reviews.

Published by
Adams Media, a division of F+W Media, Inc.
57 Littlefield Street, Avon, MA 02322. U.S.A.
www.adamsmedia.com

ISBN 10: 1-4405-0238-2
ISBN 13: 978-1-4405-0238-5
eISBN 10: 1-4405-0239-0
eISBN 13: 978-1-4405-0239-2

Printed in the United States of America.

10   9   8   7   6   5   4   3   2   1

Library of Congress Cataloging-in-Publication Data
is available from the publisher.

*This book is available at quantity discounts for bulk purchases.
For information, please call 1-800-289-0963.*

To Ellie for the practical experience; Emma, Rebel, Rosie, and Luke for the preliminary experience; and Tracey for doing it all with me.
—KW

To my family and friends.
—KB

Contents

7. Nighttime Dryness: Handling Bedwetting . . . 123

8. When Bad Accidents Happen to Good Kids . 143

9. Toilet Training a Child with Special Needs. . . 163

Acknowledgments

We have many people to thank. First, thank you to our mothers and our children for experiencing potty training with us. Thank you also to all of the mothers who shared their potty-training experiences with us and their children who made the stories worth sharing. Thank you to our editor, Brett Shanahan, for your patience and willingness to read chapter after chapter on bodily functions. Thank you to our agent, Gina Panettieri, for helping us along the way. Thank you to Jessica Williams for help with the technical side of things. Finally, thank you to Shannon Penrod for getting the project started and serving as our sounding board along the way.

Introduction

People have used different methods of potty training since the beginning of time. From Elimination Communication, through Two-Day Training, to a Dr. Spock-oriented long process approach, parents have adapted their methods of potty training in order to fit the needs of their children and the lifestyle they are living. In this book you will find a step-by-step explanation of each of these methods, how they can be practiced in daily living, as well as in-depth details to help you determine which method is best for you and your child.

Whether your child is developing on a typical schedule or has special needs, this book will guide you down a successful path to potty training. Included in explaining a variety of approaches, this book provides lists of products to help you in potty training, suggestions for supplies to take with you, and real stories from real parents about each of the methods included. Just as children develop skills at their own pace, potty training must be individualized to meet the needs of the child and parent.

As you consider each approach, it is important to remember that Rome was not built in a day, the Constitution was not written in a day, and your entire potty-training process will also not likely happen in one day either. Even if you find yourself choosing a Baby Boot Camp style of potty training in the actual practice, you will still need to spend ample time preparing yourself and your child before you take action. Knowing this, take a step back, take a deep breath, and relax. You will do fine, and your child will be potty trained. It is important for you to take a stress-free attitude into your child's potty-training experience. By maintaining low expectations in the beginning and admitting that you and your child are only human, you are allowing yourself to be pleasantly surprised by the results without unnecessary pressure on you or your child.

In addition to maintaining this relaxed mindset, you should also consider potty training as an opportunity to have a hands-on experiencing in teaching your child an important developmental lesson. In many ways potty training serves as a building block for future lessons of independence and control, and you will be helping your child establish this important foundation for upcoming stages of development. You will be working with your child through laughter and tears, frustration and joy (for you and him), and the final result will be an accomplishment you achieve together. Potty training, like his first step, his first word, and his first smile, is a monumental experience in your child's life, and you will be with him every step of the way.

CHAPTER 1

When Are You and Your Child Ready to Begin?

Children begin potty training at all different times. As you begin thinking of potty training your child, you will most likely be inundated with people advising you on the age their child started potty training and by what age your child should start as well. The fact is that every child is different. There is no cut-and-dried time period in which children should start potty training just as there is no definitive link between when a parent started potty training compared to their child.

Age and Gender Expectations

Studies have shown that girls are more likely to potty train at an early age than boys, but that does not mean this statement will hold true for all children. Typically a child will start potty training as early as twenty months or as late as three years. The age will vary, however, so it is important for parents to let their children show Mommy and Daddy when they are ready to begin potty training. If a parent starts too soon, the child will most likely not learn and the result may be many wet pants, crying children, and frustrated parents. If a child starts too late, the parent is left dealing with a frustrated child, unnecessary expenses, and a mess of diapers. On top of all this, the child may even lose interest in using the potty, forcing parents to wait even longer.

For these reasons, it's important to avoid using a number line to determine when your child should start potty training. Instead, it's important to look at specific behaviors that indicate a child is ready to begin potty training. These behaviors include:

- Verbally complaining about wet or dirty diapers
- Waking up from a nap or bedtime with a dry diaper on a regular basis
- Going to the bathroom with Mommy or Daddy
- Imitating Mommy and Daddy

These signs of bathroom interest are an invitation to the parent to begin the potty-training process. It is generally better to wait until a child is demonstrating most if not all of these signals before you begin. Let's take a closer look at what's involved.

Verbally Complaining about Wet or Dirty Diapers

From the very beginning of parenthood you have likely heard about checking for a wet or dirty diaper if your child is crying. Other parents and instructors have probably told you about how unpleasant it can be for your child to remain in a wet or dirty diaper and how they may begin communicating their displeasure at an early age. For that reason, many parents feel this sign has come long before it has. After all, if your newborn is unhappy with a wet diaper and pacified with a dry diaper, how is that not the same thing? The answer lies in the complaint.

As you have noticed by now, your baby will definitely cry to show you he is unhappy, and he may often be unhappy as a result of his diaper. When a child is ready to begin potty training, however, this complaint will take on a more sophisticated form. For example, instead of simply crying when it is time to be changed, your child may come up to you and point at his diaper. This is an indication that he not only knows why he is unhappy, but he also has a good idea of how to solve this problem. He may also try taking his diaper off by himself. Although this can be particularly unpleasant for you as a parent (depending on the nature of the diaper), it is a very good sign that he is moving toward the potty-training process. Some children will find they are unable to remove their diaper and will not be satisfied with merely pointing, and so they will come to you and tell you verbally that they have "pee peed" or "poo pooed." Regardless of which method your child uses, these are all good indications that a child is no longer satisfied with using a diaper and is instead moving toward the potty-training process.

Waking Up with a Dry Diaper

One of the trickiest parts of potty training a child can be teaching her to "hold it." During sleep times, however, children will often to hold it on their own. This most often happens after a child has associated the wet or dirty diaper with the unpleasantness that follows, and her body instinctively learns to refrain from making the diaper wet or dirty until a clean diaper is a feasible solution. Consequently, a child who has a dry diaper when she wakes up from a nap is demonstrating another sign that she may be ready to begin potty training.

As you watch for this sign, it is important to look for consistency. Staying dry overnight is usually one of the last steps for children going through potty training, but dry naptime diapers can happen long before they are actually potty trained. Likewise, a dry diaper every few days can easily be a coincidence, so it is a good idea to watch for regularity from your child. If you find your child waking up several days in a row with a dry diaper, you are ready to proceed with caution.

Imitating Mommy or Daddy

Children often learn by repetition and imitation. They speak because they are imitating the older people around them and so they frequently say words long before they know the meaning of them. At the same time, children must hear specific sounds and words multiple times in order to learn how to replicate these sounds on their own. Potty training is not all that different.

As your child grows near a possible age for potty training, it is a good idea to start taking him to the bathroom with you. You may already be doing this for safety reasons, but now is a good time to do so on a regular basis. As you use the bathroom, explain to your child what you are doing. Try changing his diaper in the bathroom and then putting your child on the toilet to help him make the association between the act of peeing, the toilet, and the diaper.

You should also involve your child in what he will likely consider the fun parts of going to the bathroom. Offer him some toilet paper as you also use toilet paper on yourself making sure you vocalize what you are doing. Next, let him flush the toilet. This is a great opportunity to make a game out of the process, which can also help maintain your child's interest in potty training. Children frequently enjoy playing with light switches and similar buttons because of the "surprise" when the light appears or disappears, and the toilet flushing has a similar effect. Another fun habit is to have him say "Goodbye!" to the toilet waste as he is flushing. All of these habits help keep your child actively involved in going to the bathroom with you even before he is ready to use the bathroom himself.

Bowel Movements

Many parents complain that their children have been successfully potty trained for a long time and yet still refuse to poop in the toilet. In actuality, potty training includes all aspects of going to the bathroom, so the process isn't officially complete until your child will poop and pee in the toilet. Understanding that potty training isn't done yet will help you maintain patience and understanding as you and your child work together to complete this stage in her development.

 Alert

> Constipation can make it difficult for your child to poop in a toilet. Because constipation involves hard, often painful bowel movements, the child is less likely to spend the time on the toilet and more likely to want to avoid bowel movements altogether. Increasing fluids and fiber in your child's diet can help her overcome her constipation. If this does not work, consult your pediatrician about using a stool softener to put an end to her constipation.

Bowel movements are often the most complicated part of potty training. Disposable diapers have advanced so far as to eliminate most of the sensation of a wet diaper, and peeing occurs with such frequency that's it's easy to expedite a toddler's familiarity with peeing into a toilet or potty chair. Bowel movements, however, are different altogether.

The most obvious difference with bowel movements is that a toddler always knows when she has pooped. There is no way to create a diaper that removes the bowel movement from the toddler's skin, so the sensation is immediate. Similarly, bowel movements typically only occur once or twice per day for a toddler, whereas a child can pee an almost unlimited number of times per day. For this reason there are several additional steps to take to help your child adjust to pooping in a toilet.

- **Step 1:** When your child has pooped in her diaper, empty the diaper into the toilet while your child watches. This practice is not unlike potty training a dog, and with good reason: it works! Showing your child the proper place to put poop will encourage her to want to put the poop there herself. This will motivate her to poop in the potty and not in her diaper.
- **Step 2:** Show your child books or movies that involve potty training. There are several options available that show children how other children or their favorite cartoon characters are also learning how to use the potty. Using books and media can help make the process fun for your child, maintain their interest in learning to use the potty, and ultimately help them feel more like a big kid when they are done potty training.

- **Step 3:** Watch for problems with constipation. Many children are afraid of or uncomfortable with pooping in a toilet, so they will hold it for as long as they can. Holding it too long can result in constipation, which is painful for the child and difficult for the parent. If you are patient with this stage of potty training, you are more likely to successfully achieve a diaper-free child without encountering constipation.

🛑 Alert

Preparing everyone involved often includes babysitters, grandparents, daycare providers, and any other caregiver who may help you take care of your child. Making a list of the people involved can help you remember who you need to talk to and how much information you need to give them so that everyone can participate in your child's potty training.

Prepare Yourself First

Before you start potty training, you should also start considering the equipment that will best work for your child in your home, the time that is involved, and the ways your routine will likely change as you make potty training a new priority in your day. Potty training cannot be a part-time process, so it is important to make sure you are fully prepared to begin potty training before you even start.

Another key step in potty training is making sure everyone around you is involved. Once you begin, it can be a big step backward to take a diaper-free child and put her in a Pull-Up for a day. At the same time, it can be very difficult for you to be around your child twenty-four hours per day, so it is important to make sure everyone is on board.

In short, as important as it is to make sure your child is ready to begin potty training before you get started, it is equally important to make sure that you are prepared. Below are some questions to ask yourself to determine if you are ready to potty train your child.

Portable Potty Chair or Booster Seat for the Toilet?

There are several brands of potty chairs available; some sing, some make flushing noises, and some even cheer for your child if he uses the potty correctly. Some special seats are designed to fit on your toilet already regardless of size or shape. It is important for you to decide what works best for you and your child before you begin the process. Consider the size of your child and whether the potential transition from a potty chair to a step stool will help you in the future. Because all children and all parents are different, this book will not aim to endorse any one brand or style of potty-training equipment. Instead, you should examine your home and your child and find what works best for you.

More than One Potty?

It can take considerable time before a child is ready to "hold it." For this reason, you may need to consider having multiple potty-training tools available for your child. This will become more important as you digest the upcoming chapters of this book and decide which method will work best for you. For example, the Baby Boot Camp method requires ready-made access to a potty chair at all times while a slower method may allow your child to learn where one particular potty is available so he understands he needs to reach that potty in time. As you choose a method, make sure you are prepared to purchase the necessary equipment for that method.

Do You Have the Time to Consistently Take Your Child to the Bathroom?

As previously stated and will surely be stated again, potty training is not a part-time process. As a parent, it is important to make sure you are ready to take your child to the bathroom whenever it is necessary. Accidents will happen, but fewer accidents and faster learning will take place if you are consistently ready to listen to and assist your child whenever he is ready to use the potty.

Are Day Care Workers Ready and Willing to Assist?

This section is particularly important to the working parent. Your child may be ready to potty train as early as eighteen months or as late as thirty-six months. Regardless of when they are ready, it is absolutely necessary for your day care provider to be equally cooperative. If and when you are ready to begin potty training at home, the day care must also be available to listen to your child, take him or her to the potty when necessary, and follow whatever system or schedule you set up. However, you as the parent must also remember that your child is probably not the only one at your day care. To best work around the other children, consider partnering with the teachers. Learn what programs or schedules they have in place, and try to adapt to their system as well. Compromise is key when multiple adults are involved in potty training a child.

Any Major Trips Planned Soon?

Vacations are a wonderful time for family bonding, but they can also interfere with the potty-training process. It is difficult and can be impossible for toddlers to maintain potty-training practices when on airplanes or long car rides. Whether it be a long-running "Fasten Seatbelt" sign on a plane or a major gap between rest stations on the road, traveling usually requires long periods where a child is unable to go to the bathroom. At the same time, reverting to a pull-up diaper as a preventative measure can run the risk of encouraging your child to regress to an earlier stage of potty training. For all these reasons, it is usually best to wait to begin potty training until you have plenty of time to finish the process and teach your child to "hold it" before such holding is required.

Does Your Child Spend Significant Time Periods with Grandparents or a Babysitter?

In the best of all situations, grandparents and babysitters already have experience potty training young toddlers. However, experience is not always enough. Just as each child is unique in when he will begin potty training, each child is unique in how willing he is to participate in potty-training practices, communicate his needs, and use bathroom facilities different than what they have at home. Similarly, grandparents and babysitters must be prepared to take part in the potty training if your child is with them on a regular basis or for an extended period of time. All caregivers involved must be prepared for accidents, frequent trips to the bathroom, sudden demands to use the bathroom, and so much more. Toddlers typically require going to the bathroom more often than adults, but they may also ask to go more often simply because it is a new and interesting experience. If they are rewarded when they go to the bathroom, they may ask to go more often simply so they may receive their reward. All toddlers will have an accident at some point during or even after the potty-training process. As you prepare to potty train, it is your responsibility as the parent to make sure all caregivers involved are ready, willing, and able to fulfill their role in the potty-training process.

Have You Made the Transition from a Crib to a Toddler Bed?

Once your child has left his crib, it is important to consider how this will affect his potty-training process. If you are using a portable potty chair, you may choose to leave it in his room for him to use unassisted during the night. However, this can make things messier, particularly if you have a son. For hygienic reasons, most pediatricians recommend keeping all bathroom practices outside of the bedroom and in a supervised environment, especially in the beginning. If your child is still in a crib, this puts the responsibility on you as the parent to get up during the night when your child calls to you to go to the bathroom. People of all ages typically find themselves in a deep sleep where using the restroom is not necessary in the middle of the night, but there is still no one hard and fast rule regarding nighttime bathroom practices. Using a mattress pad and a nighttime diaper can ease the transition out of a diaper in the beginning while still maintaining a sanitary environment.

 **Essential**

Another aspect of preparing yourself and other caregivers for potty training is being willing to take a son into the women's restroom or a daughter into the men's restroom. For safety and assistance reasons, it will be many years before your child will be able to use a public restroom by himself. Although more and more public venues are providing family-friendly restrooms, it will still be necessary at some point for your child to enter the opposite gender's restroom.

Are You Prepared for Accidents?

If you cannot answer "yes" to this question, you are not ready to begin potty training. You will most likely be inundated with stories about the child who had accidents till he was twelve just as much as you will be cornered with stories about the child with the perfect potty-training experience who never had an accident. There is something you should know now: memories are forgiving things. Every child will have an accident at some point. Whether it is during the night, in the middle of the shopping mall, or at the climax of the movie you have been waiting months to see, every child will have an accident. Some children will take considerably longer than others to finish potty training, while some will take to it right away and then unexpectedly have an accident when they are five years old. The only guarantee in potty training is that there are no guarantees. You as the parent must be ready both mentally and physically for accidents.

 Fact

Remember that accidents can be pee, poop, or both. Diarrhea in particular can cause an inordinate number of problems. In addition to carrying the traditional tools to clean up and move on from an accident, you may want to consider carrying antibacterial cleanser for your hands, a spot remover laundry spray or stick for your child's clothes, and rash cream for your child's bottom. Preparation is key to minimizing and managing any accident your child may have.

Mentally, it is important to make sure you do not grow angry with your child. Yelling, scolding, and punishing will only add to the humiliation and discomfort the child is already feeling. Physically, you need to be prepared for a mess the same way you have been all along with diapers. Even after you have finished potty training, you should still keep a change of clothes, diaper wipes, and a plastic bag (for the soiled clothing) available at all times. The best offense is a good defense, and the more prepared you are for an accident, the less it will upset both you and your child.

Are You Prepared for the Initial Cost Burden?

While it is true that discontinuing diaper use can bring some financial relief to your family, the reprieve does not come right away. First, training diapers are typically more expensive than traditional diapers. Similarly, there are scads of potty chairs, toilet paper, and toilet-style booster seats all designed to help you with your potty-training process. While none of these products are absolutely necessary for potty training, many people have found the process easier with the use of a step, a booster seat, or a separate potty chair to help their child use a toilet. Special toilet paper that indicates how much your child should use through cute pictures may save you from hours of plunging and cleanup, but it, too, will be more expensive than regular toilet paper. If you know ahead of time that you want to use products to help you or even if you think you may feel so inclined, it is worth your time to investigate how much these products cost before you begin potty training.

Are There Infants in Your Family or Will There Be One Soon?

A baby is always a blessing but, as you know by now, a baby is also a lot of work. A baby will take away a size-able portion of your time and attention from your toddler. This will affect your potty training in two ways. First, you will have fewer opportunities to help your child with potty training. Because potty training is a new experience for any toddler, you must be prepared for sudden demands to use the restroom, extended periods of time on the toilet or potty chair, and, of course, the unexpected accidents. Caring for an infant at the same time can make all of these aspects of potty training more difficult. The second effect of an infant on potty training comes in the form of regression. It is not at all unusual for a toddler to associate the infantile behavior of the new baby with the outpouring of love and attention that you show your new child. Your toddler may respond by reverting to his own infantile behavior in the form of crying, thumb-sucking, increased demands for attention, and, of course, accidents. This does not mean that is impossible to potty train a toddler when you have an infant. If that were true, families would space their children by four years apart or more. Instead, it simply means that you should spend time considering how the new addition to your family may affect your potty-training progress. As always, the more prepared you are for the possibilities, the more able you will be to overcome any obstacles in a timely and efficient manner.

Are You Prepared for the Increase in Laundry?

As you know by now, accidents will happen. Accidents will affect your child's pants, underpants, sheets, blankets, and more. When your child was an infant you gained early exposure to the dramatic increase in laundry that comes with having a baby. Now that your child is approaching the potty-training stage, the laundry will increase once again. This section is not designed to put you off of potty training, but is instead a gentle reminder of a change you should anticipate as you begin potty training. With luck and the help of this book, your potty-training period will be short and you will soon find yourself back to a normal load of laundry, with the added bonus of a diaper-free child!

CHAPTER 2

Getting Started

· ·

It is important that you keep a positive attitude as you approach each aspect of potty training. There will be days when your angelic toddler is compliant with every request. Other days won't be so heavenly and you'll wonder if it's really so bad to send your child to middle school in diapers. Remember, your child will be potty trained. So for now, just take a deep breath, relax, and keep a smile on your face. In order to proceed, it is necessary to talk about your toddler's growth and development. For many, this will be the first time you have heard some of these terms. Don't worry; this will not be a lengthy lesson in psychology. However, it is critical to know the natural development of your child as she ages.

· ·

Stages of Development

Erik Erikson (1902–1994) was a developmental psychologist known for his work in social theory. Erikson's child development theory built on the work of Sigmund Freud, expanding Freud's five stages of psychosexual development into eight stages of development that span one's life in its entirety—birth through death. Much of what is known about human development and ego is based on his work. In fact, Erikson was the first psychologist to describe the term "identity crisis." In this chapter you will learn about the first two stages and how they pertain to your child.

First Stage

As an infant (birth through one year), your child's developmental task, according to Erikson, was establishing Trust versus Mistrust. She was fully dependent on you for meeting all of her needs. She learned the world around her through your interactions with her. The main concern of the infant is whether or not her environment is secure and supportive. Therefore, your role during her infancy was to provide warmth, food, shelter, comfort, affection, and basic care. When these basic needs were provided, she learned to trust you and other caregivers.

Second Stage

Now, as a toddler (two to three years old), your child has moved beyond establishing trust. She now has an idea of the world around her and is ready to explore. Her task during this phase of development is establishing Autonomy versus Shame and Doubt. The primary concern of the toddler is whether she can do things by herself or if she must rely on others. This is the age where your child learns to exert her will. Likely you have seen some of this exertion of will through temper tantrums, refusals to eat, and the frequent favorite word of the toddler, "NO!" You can easily see why potty training is best left for this stage of psychological development. Prior to this age, your child was more an extension of you instead of an independent being.

Do not be mistaken. Although this stage is characterized by your toddler's quest for independence, she still relies on you for safety and security. She knows that you are her provider. Even though she learned that you are the stability in her life when she was only an infant, she is now ready to explore her surroundings.

Physically, the task of potty training will be her single greatest accomplishment during this phase as it marks a huge step toward achieving her autonomy. Parents are able to foster autonomy through demonstrating patience and support. Conversely, parents who are restrictive or overly cautious instill feelings of doubt. These children grow to be reluctant to try new things. Have you seen the child who refuses to go into the gym class while retreating behind her mother's legs? Encouraging self-sufficient behavior helps your toddler feel confident in her ability to attempt the next task. She will be eager to show you everything she can do by herself. Things like feeding herself, washing herself, dressing herself, and going to the potty are all tasks your toddler will master during the next couple of years. Parents and caregivers can thwart the efforts of a well-intentioned toddler when they demand too much too soon. They may also deflate the toddler's self-esteem when they prohibit her from performing tasks independently or ridiculing her when she is unsuccessful.

Children develop at different rates, and so they must be evaluated independent of other children, even if they are in the same family. Potty training comprises such a large component of developing independence that it must be seriously considered prior to beginning.

How Development Affects Potty Training

Now that you have had a brief discussion of development, it is time to get into the issue at hand: potty training. There are several factors that influence a child's schedule for potty training. One is gender, as girls typically master most skills earlier than boys. For example, in their 2008 article "Toilet Training," Beth A. Choby and Shefaa George state that remaining free from overnight bowel movement is typically seen around twenty-two months in little girls but not until approximately twenty-five months in boys. Another consideration is whether or not your child has the ability to pull up underwear or training pants. Again, according to Choby and Shefaa, girls usually master this task about four months earlier than boys, or just before thirty months. A third factor influencing potty training is whether or not your child attends day care. Toddlers attending day care facilities are often encouraged to begin potty training around the age of twenty-four months regardless of individual readiness. This is often due to limited classroom space or enrollment, promotion to older toddler rooms, and teacher motivation. If you are considering beginning potty training, discuss it with your child care provider so that routines may be carried out while she is at day care. Many times the day care teacher or babysitter has additional information that you may not have considered in your decision. This period of development is extremely frustrating for parents who are diligent in potty training at home but have no support from their child care provider.

Tools of the Trade

Once you decide which method you will use for potty training (methods will be discussed in later chapters of this book), you may want to motivate your child with a visual aid. Several different dolls come with bottles and "diapers" that are great for showing your child the process of potty training. There are also many books and videos that may stimulate your child to become more compliant with the whole potty-training process. Some of these aids are quite simple and geared more toward the younger potty trainer, while others are a bit more detailed.

Whether or not you decide to use any visual aids, this is a great opportunity to remind you to make this process fun. The more relaxed you are, the better your experience will be. Remember, your child has never done this before. He needs you to be supportive.

> **JESSE, father to Lydia, 18 months:**
> "My daughter began taking a bath in the big bathtub when she was about twelve months old, and she absolutely loved taking her doll into the bath with her. As I watched her play with and 'take care of' her doll, I realized how much more we could be learning during bath time. I soon introduced a doll that was designed to help with potty training. If you dunked the doll in the water, the doll would take some of the water into her body. As soon as my daughter was done in the bath, I put her doll on the toilet and showed her how the doll was 'going potty.' My daughter wanted to be just like her doll, so she started using the potty as well!"

Introducing the Potty Chair

There is no required equipment for potty training other than a potty, but certain tools can help make the process that much smoother. Potty chairs can be found in all shapes and sizes, many of which are intended to encourage your toddler to stay put until the mission is accomplished. Potty chairs can be very low-tech; some in fact, are not a potty chair at all but an adapter ring for the regular commode that prevents your child from falling in. Newer models play music once urination begins, thereby encouraging your child to continue. (One disadvantage to this particular type of potty chair is that your child may turn to find the source of the music, which then changes the direction of the stream of urine.)

One factor to consider in choosing the type of potty your child will use is her size or height. Taller children will have an easier time with the adapter ring-fitted adult toilet or larger potty chair whereas shorter children will have greater success with the smaller potty chair. The reason for this is the position of the legs as they sit on the chair. Body position is a key factor during a bowel movement; children need to be able to have their feet on the floor with their knees at a right angle during bowel movements. It is likely that, if your toddler is using the adult potty, she will need a stool placed below her feet to give her stability.

 Fact

The cost of potty chairs and adaptive devices ranges from around $9 to $30. Although these prices are reasonable, if you are on a tight budget, garage sales are a great place to find bargains on potty chairs. You may want to consider taking your child along as you shop for a potty chair.

It is important to realize when selecting your toddler's potty chair how much cleaning or maintenance is required. Most potty chairs have a removable collection device that must be emptied and cleaned following each trip to the potty. The lower-tech items, such as the potty seat, only need to be wiped down with bathroom cleanser like you would a regular commode seat.

There are several other features to consider as you choose your child's potty chair or seat. One is the stability of the chair. You must anticipate your little one will become bored with sitting and begin to move around on the chair. Look for a chair that will not tip as your child leans in different directions.

Another important feature is a splashguard. Little boys are not the best at remembering to aim their urine streams, and therefore a splashguard is an invaluable time saving device when it comes to cleaning the bathroom floor. The splashguard is not without its own potential hazard, since some potty chair models do not have padding. What that means is that your son may be scratched or injured if he is leans too far forward or there is not enough room between him and the splashguard.

In addition, a padded seat is far more comfortable than a non-padded seat. Another feature to look for is a conversion or transition option. Some of the more expensive models of potty chairs are also a stepstool, while others will convert to a potty seat once the chair is no longer necessary.

No matter which potty chair or potty seat you and your toddler select, you may see some resistance to use it once you get home. Just as she is picky about what she eats, she may be equally picky about where she sits to poop. Keep in mind, though, that everything is temporary. Ultimately you will both have great success.

Disposable Briefs, Underwear, or Training Pants

Physical readiness for potty training is just as important as mental or emotional readiness for potty training. It is important that your toddler has the capability of dressing and undressing himself as he rushes to the potty. Clothing, therefore, should be easily removable with elastic waistbands and Velcro instead of snaps and zippers. Additionally, be sure that your child's pants are not tight or restrictive. Pulling down tight pants may waste valuable seconds as he tries to avoid an accident.

Essential

There is really no "wrong" choice when it comes to disposable briefs. Cost tends to be the primary consideration when it comes to disposable briefs. Just as with diapers, there are name brand and generic or store brand choices with price differences similar to diaper pricing.

Toddlers look forward to the day they begin to wear "big boy" underwear or "big girl" panties. Because accidents are going to happen, it's a good idea to begin the process while your child is in diapers. Once he has had several days of success, you may wish to use disposable briefs to make trips to the restroom easier. Once your child is using the toilet, he will be less than cooperative when placed on the changing table for a new diaper.

Disposable briefs are available in several varieties, and most are gender specific with princesses for girls and trucks for boys. They may have a highly absorbent layer that wicks all moisture from the skin, and this can be a big disadvantage since your child may not feel the wetness that cues his need to avoid accidents. Others have special layers that leave just enough moisture on the skin or change temperature so that, theoretically, the child will recognize the need to get to a toilet. Some of the briefs have figures on the front of the brief that fade as they become soiled, alerting parents to change the brief.

Many parents choose to stay with diapers until they are able to convert completely to underwear, and this is often a big incentive for the aspiring superhero underwear or fairytale princess panty-wearer. On the other hand, an advantage to placing your child in panties or underwear before that is the immediate recognition of an accident. You could choose to use the heavier cloth training pants first; but know there is really no advantage to this other than a little greater absorbency in the crotch. This is helpful for catching those small dribbles that do not necessarily support a full underwear change. If you have concerns about leaking, you may use a plastic pant or waterproof diaper cover over the training pants.

Keep in mind that you'll be changing underwear several times a day if you decide to put your potty-training toddler into big boy or girl underwear, and these frequent changes may increase frustration for parents as well as the toddler. (Remember the discussion in Chapter 1 about increased laundry expectations?) You should probably come to terms with the idea that several pairs may be tossed out with the trash when they are too soiled. Along that same vein, avoid punishing your child for accidents. Accidents *will* happen (see Chapter 8).

🅔❗ Alert

Training Tip: Keep clean underwear or disposable briefs in the bathroom instead of the bedroom. This will promote a sense of independence in your toddler as he learns to take care of accidents.

New Words

Now that you are moving forward with potty training, it is important to keep terminology consistent when it comes to going to the restroom. This process actually begins from birth as you talk to your infant while changing her diaper. There are no right or wrong words for the process of elimination; some parents chose to use words that are slang such as "pee," "tee tee," "pee pee," "potty," "poo," "poop," or "stinky." Other parents choose to be more technically correct and use terms such as urinate and defecate.

Now that you have thought about bodily functions, you may want to consider what you will call body parts. This is another area where slang words are frequently used when children are infants and toddlers. Little boys may use words like "privates," "boy parts," or "pee pee" for penis while little girls may use words such as "tu-tu," "bottom," or "privates" for vagina. Again, consistency is the key for success.

If you decide to use slang words, it is important to teach your child the correct terminology once she is school age. A second grade girl at her first sleepover may be embarrassed to tell her friend's mother that her "tu-tu" hurts if she does not know the right way to say it.

> **KIM, mother of Shelby, Morgan, Barrett, and Erin:**
> "My friend's mother was a nurse. When we were in nursing school, she shared that often when she was a little girl and had friends over they would run through the house on the way to the restroom shouting they needed to 'pee' or 'poop.' This would prompt a musical reply by her mom, 'ur-i-naaate' or 'def-e-caaate.'"

Potty Talk

Uncle Jeff may find it extremely entertaining when his two year old nephew announces his need to take a "crap" or "piss" or other words that border curse words, but these words are extremely offensive and should not be encouraged. Other parents may not be eager to have their children play with a child who uses such terms either.

Most toddlers at some point exercise their boundary pushing skills by becoming sassy. After a long week at day care, your child may come home to call you a "doo-doo head" as he giggles uncontrollably. Your job is to remain calm, cool, and collected. (Hopefully he has done this while you are driving so he cannot see your appalled expression.) This is a time to put your best acting skills to use. Take a deep breath before your respond, because he is more likely to try it again if you respond in shock or anger.

While you don't want to respond with laughter, anger, or frustration, you do want to address with your toddler that his language is not acceptable outside the bathroom. You may wish to have your child repeat all of the "potty" terms he knows so that you can emphasize that words on his list are to be used in the bathroom only. This does two things for your toddler: now he knows the boundary you have for him when it comes to "potty talk," and he also knows that you love him enough to be patient for such a conversation instead of punishing him for something he had no idea was so wrong.

If your child continues to use inappropriate language or calls people names, it is important to be very specific and firm as you explain which words or names are offensive. It is also important to begin teaching him about the feelings of others, so let him know how much it hurts your feelings when he calls you names. Let him know that his behavior is not acceptable, but at the same time offer alternative words or phrases he may use when he is angry or frustrated. For example, you can tell him it's okay to say things like, "That makes me mad" or "I am mad at you." Reassure him that being angry or frustrated is okay, but he must be kind to others.

Keeping It Clean

During the toddler years, it is not unusual to find your child with her hand in her diaper without any evidence of being disgusted by the waste product on her fingers. This is the reason most toddlers are oblivious to the idea of potty training until their resourceful parents begin the process. However, if you notice that your child frequently tells you when she has a wet diaper or you find her with her diaper off because it is dirty, you are definitely ready to begin potty training.

In fact, if you do find your child playing with her stool, use restraint in your response; she has no idea how disgusting her poop is to adults. Communicate to your child that playing with stool is not acceptable and thoroughly clean her up. Wash her hands with soap and water for about fifteen to twenty seconds, and be sure you clean under her fingernails as well.

EMILY, mother of Brooke and Ethan:
"I went upstairs one afternoon to check on our eighteen-month-old daughter after a nap. I walked in to find her standing in her crib finger painting . . . with her dirty diaper beside her. I quietly closed the door and yelled for my husband to head upstairs. I left to buy a potty chair."

Along with the recognition of being wet or dirty, your toddler will need to be prompted on steps to take for personal hygiene after she uses the potty. The habits she develops now will last for her lifetime, so it is important to start this process from the beginning. You will teach everything from hand washing to flushing to wiping up splashes around the sink as well as the toilet seat. You will also want to include raising and lowering the toilet seat and paying attention to the urine stream for little boys so they avoid spraying the walls or floor.

One way parents can help their sons with aim is by creating targets in the toilet for "sinking" with the stream of urine. This may be accomplished by sprinkling a few Cheerios in the water or tearing small bits of tissue paper and placing them in the water. These aids will not only help your toddler learn how to focus his stream of urine to reduce the mess and cleanup time, but the aids will also help make a game out of potty training. Sinking cereal can only happen when it is time to pee, so he will be more likely to watch for signs that he needs to go to the bathroom—and is ready to play his game again.

Hand Washing

Good hygiene begins with basic hand washing. Not only does proper hand washing technique keep your child's hands clean, but it also prevents disease. Hand washing may be achieved by washing with regular soap and water or by using alcohol-based, no rinse cleansers. These cleansers are a good alternative to soap and water, and most provide moisturizers to prevent dry hands as well as antibacterial coverage for most viruses and bacteria. They are great for use on the go at places like the park, the grocery store, church, and restaurants where water and soap are not easily accessible. The only time soap and water is absolutely recommended over alcohol-based cleansers is when hands have become contaminated or soiled with body fluids like urine, stool, blood, mucus, etc. Thus, following a trip to the bathroom, your toddler needs a soap and water wash. Teach your child from the beginning how to thoroughly clean her hands. Here are the five steps:

1. Wet hands
2. Apply soap (liquid or foam cleanser is preferred over bar soap)
3. Rub hands together, creating friction between the fingers, for about fifteen seconds (Singing or humming the "Happy Birthday" song is just the right amount of time and is fun for your child.)
4. Rinse hands well with water
5. Dry hands using a clean towel

A note on antibacterial cleansers: you can purchase almost everything in an antibacterial form these days. From surface cleansers to hand soaps to shoes with antibacterial liners, almost every household cleaning product has been developed in an antibacterial form. Parents, doctors, and hygiene experts have begun focusing more on the abundant use of antibacterial cleansers and the population's increasing resistance of bacteria in the environment. This phenomenon is similar to what has been recognized in over-the-counter lice insecticides and antibiotics. It is recommended, therefore, that plain soap and water, when used appropriately, are adequate for keeping your toddler's germs in check.

Wiping
Perineal hygiene is paramount during potty training. Clean skin reduces odor, skin irritation, infection, and the

staining of underwear. Girls are particularly susceptible to local skin irritation when they are not completely clean. In addition, lingering residue from bowel movements can increase the potential for urinary tract infections in girls. Boys have less potential for urinary tract infections, but may be equally irritated when not clean.

Wiping is a new task for toddlers, and not one that comes naturally. This will take patient instruction on your part, but don't worry; even school-aged children and teenagers have challenges estimating the right amount of toilet paper for the job. Toddlers seem to start by using either too much or not enough toilet paper, and each comes with its own hazards. Too much toilet paper is likely going to cause flushing difficulties or toilet clogs, while too little will cause seriously dirty hands. Dirty hands may be a cause for panic in the toddler who does not like to be dirty. This creates a fear she will need to overcome.

By anatomical default, boys have an easier time learning to wipe since only one area becomes dirty. Their challenge is related to determining whether or not they are completely clean following a bowel movement. You will more than likely find that you want to follow up for the first few months of potty training to be sure he has been successful in cleaning up after a trip to the bathroom. Uncircumcised boys have an additional task to master, so you will need to teach your son to gently retract the foreskin to clean the tip of the penis. This is best accomplished at bath time, although it can be done at any time. Remember to push the foreskin back around the tip of the penis after cleansing. Failure to do this could cause a painful condition called phimosis, which potentially could warrant surgical intervention.

Girls generally have a more difficult time learning the fine art of wiping. Girls should wipe from front to back and then drop their tissue in the toilet. Positioning may be difficult in smaller children since they cannot reach from front to back easily. Some moms find it easier to have their daughters use more of a "pushing" motion where the toddler holds the toilet paper in her hand between her legs, pushes the paper to wipe and drops the paper once she reaches her anus. For this reason, your daughter should sit with her legs slightly spread apart on the commode instead of with her knees together.

No matter whether you are teaching a boy or girl wiping techniques, all children need to be taught to continue to wipe until they see no more stool on the tissue. This may warrant the use of wet wipes. If you decide to try wet wipes, be sure to find wipes that are flushable. You may also want to put these in an area of the bathroom that deter overuse. Too much of a good thing can be a problem too.

Flushing

Flushing the potty is a necessary step to teach your child. Some children are afraid of the loud noise and do not want to be involved in the process, while others can't wait to push the magic button that takes the poop and paper away. Some parents will see a slight increase in their water bill as they find their toddler flushing for fun. Be sure to use a toilet lid safety latch to prevent the flushing of toys, cellular phones, and other basic items found around your house that are not intended for bathroom fun.

Diaper Rash

Diaper rash may be characterized by increased redness around the labia or anus. It may be minor or major, but it is often painful for the child. The rash may be red and smooth resembling a scraped knee, or it may be red and bumpy resembling pimples or blisters. If your child experiences diaper rash, using a zinc oxide-based cream or ointment will help heal the skin. In order to have the best result, you must apply the cream with each trip to the toilet. It may be important to ensure that she has cream in place prior to urination or bowel movements in order to reduce discomfort associated with each elimination process.

In many cases of prolonged (more than three days) diaper rash, children will also have an over growth of yeast. When a yeast (also called *Candida*) rash is present, it often looks like a solid red rash with small red bumps migrating from the edges. This type of rash often includes the inguinal folds (skin in the creases) instead of just the convex surfaces (rounded areas) of the buttocks. Avoid the use of cornstarch, may cause a yeast infection to worsen, and powders with a yeast rash. If you are concerned that your child has developed a yeast infection or rash, over-the-counter preparations may not be helpful. For all diaper rashes lasting more than three days, contact your health care provider.

CHAPTER 3

Starting with Day One: Elimination Communication

Elimination Communication (EC), also known as Infant Potty Training or Natural Infant Hygiene, is a natural, practical way to begin potty training far earlier than traditional toilet training techniques allow. EC can begin as early as birth or as late as parents are comfortable, but parents typically begin using EC between birth and four months. This is a clean, all natural way to teach your child from the beginning how to recognize and control his bodily functions.

What Is Elimination Communication?

Elimination Communication focuses on caregivers recognizing an infant's signals and having him pee or poop in a toilet bowl or waste container rather than in a diaper. Using sounds and signals to communicate between the parent and infant works to strengthen the bond, increases communication, and ultimately makes for a smoother transition into final potty training. Although your child will not be eliminating waste independently until he is fully mobile, he will be more likely to potty train faster and use bathroom facilities independently at an earlier age if you begin with EC.

How Does EC Work?

Elimination Communication links to a timeless practice, still popular in Europe and Asia, where parents and caregivers learn to watch and listen to infants when it comes time to pee or poop. By focusing more directly on your baby's bathroom needs in much the same way you focus on your baby's nutrition needs, you can enable yourself to avoid common, everyday parenting issues such as fussy babies, dirty diapers, leaky diapers, and more. EC follows several simple steps to help parents and infants adapt naturally to what has always been a natural progression toward potty training.

Step 1: Know Your Baby

Many parents see this step and they feel inclined to move on right away. Of course you know your baby! It is your baby, after all. However, EC requires you to know your baby on a more intimate level than diapered babies. For EC to work, you need to know your baby's routine in terms of eating and sleeping as well as peeing and pooping. How often is she going to the bathroom? How long does she wait after eating before she eliminates waste from her system? How often does she pee or poop while sleeping? The answers to all of these questions will help you to know ahead of time when to watch for your baby's bathroom signals.

ⓔ✱ Essential

Many mothers wonder why they have not heard of Elimination Communication before. While EC is a commonly used practice in some cultures, it is still not necessarily a recommended practice for modern-day families in the United States. Pediatricians vary on whether or not they endorse this practice, so there is no one easy answer as to whether or not Elimination Communication is better or worse than traditional potty training.

You also need to get to know your baby's signals. Many parents report babies kicking their legs, kicking off blankets, waking from a deep sleep, flaring their nostrils, refusing to latch on when nursing, squirming, passing gas, unexplained crying, and intense looks of concentration as signs their children are preparing to eliminate. All of these signs are common in infants, but it is important that you watch for your own child's signals. There is no one universal signal that will indicate when an infant is preparing to eliminate. As you focus more on your child's signals and needs, however, you will become more aware of which unique signals work for her.

🅔 Alert

Not all mothers will pick up on their children's signals right away. It takes time and practice to learn when your baby is signaling and what each signal means. Don't get discouraged if it takes you weeks or even months to learn how your baby communicates. At the same time, you should be prepared for your baby's signals to change as she develops and matures.

Step 2: Use an Elimination Container

Once you have become aware of your child's signals, it is time to begin using a toilet or basin. As soon as you notice your child signaling that she is going to eliminate, remove any pants, diapers, or blankets that may be in the way. Then, hold your child over the elimination container so she can proceed.

The way you hold your child is particularly important. Parents often feel inclined to hold their children at arms' length with the child's legs dangling. In other words, parents usually want the maximum distance possible between the waste and themselves. While it may be ideal for you to minimize your contact with your child's pee or poop, such a hold will more than likely frighten your child, making her either too nervous to eliminate or else so nervous that she eliminates out of fear rather than out of a natural need. The lesson of when and where to pee or poop is lost on a child held in this fashion.

Instead, you should look for a hold that provides security for the baby and comfort for you. You should find a way to hold your child that keeps her feeling safe and protected as she learns this new lesson about peeing and pooping. Try cradling her behind her shoulders and under her knees. If that doesn't work, consider waiting until she has enough muscle control to allow you to hold her under her arms, making sure to support her head, and allowing her to assume a sitting position on your basin. As you and your infant progress with EC, you will instinctively find the hold that works best for you.

Your baby won't learn right away when it is time to pee or poop, so you want to make sure you are prepared to hold her in a particular place for several minutes. Many parents have reported success using the same potty chairs that other parents use for potty-training toddlers, while other parents move right to the toilet. Still other parents select a smaller plastic basin or bowl that they designate as the "elimination container." Whichever container you choose is up to you, but it is important to see how certain sizes and materials may benefit your baby.

Remember that there is no "standard" elimination container; find one that works best for you and your baby, experimenting with several different ones if need be. Smaller containers allow you to hold your child in such a way that she grows accustomed to wrapping her legs on the sides of the container in much the same way she will when she uses a regular toilet. Mobile potty chairs or plastic containers are more accessible for you as a parent, although they are messier to clean and care for than a typical toilet. Porcelain toilet bowls tend to be colder, which will increase the discomfort level for some infants as you begin elimination communication.

 Fact

As you choose your elimination container, you need to remember that one of the goals of EC is proper hygiene. In addition to finding a container that is safe and comfortable for you and your baby, you also need to be prepared to clean and sanitize this container after each use. Most basic dishwashing and house cleaning products will work to clean and sanitize your container.

Step 3: Communicate with Your Child

As you work on EC with your child, you will listen for sounds from her that indicate she is ready to go to the bathroom. At the same time, you can also use sounds to show her you are ready for her to begin eliminating. These sounds not only work to help the EC process, but also encourage your child to use sounds as a means to communicate with you as the parent at an earlier age, without necessarily resorting to crying.

Once you have begun to hold your child over the basin, begin making a soft sound in her ear. Many parents report success with sounds that imitate the sound of a water flow, such as "sssssss" or "pepepepe." The idea here is that your child will begin to associate this sound with the time to release her bladder and move her bowels. In the beginning, this will work to help her know when you are ready. You can begin scheduling times for her to go to the bathroom much the same way you might ask your older child to use the bathroom before you leave the house. You are communicating to your infant you are ready for her to eliminate (even if she is not). As your child progresses, you will soon notice her using these sounds to communicate back to you when she needs to go to the bathroom. This is another sign that you have strengthened your bond with your child and increased her level of communication. Working with her on one of her most basic needs benefits both you and your child on multiple fronts.

Step 4: Maintain a Relaxed, Flexible, and Positive Attitude

EC is just like potty training in that it can be frustrating for the parent and for the infant. However, it is absolutely necessary for you to stay calm and uplifting throughout the process. Messes are a natural part of any infant's life—regardless of whether you use EC or not—so don't get upset. Your infant will sense your discomfort or frustration, and you will see a corresponding response from her. For these reasons, it is important to remember that accidents will happen. Your baby will need you to be flexible about when she eliminates, how she eliminates, and how quickly she picks up on the methods you've chosen. She will also need you to maintain a positive attitude about her progress. EC experts typically discourage parents from using either punishments or rewards when training your child, but it is still important to maintain an attitude that will work for both you and your infant. Remember, she will take her cues from you on attitude just as much as they will about feeding, eliminating, and more. You are her leader in every way, and, after all, she is brand new here!

Obstacles to EC

Elimination Communication is not right for everyone. Parents who choose to use EC are most often people who practice Attachment Parenting or Continuum Concept Parenting. Attachment Parenting typically involves keeping the baby on the parent's body with a sling or similar hold, extending nursing schedules, and co-sleeping. This does not mean that a parent using EC must also follow all parts of the Attachment Parenting regimen, but many aspects of EC fit in better with a parent who is constantly and consistently with his or her child.

Similarly, EC is made more difficult by alternative schedules. If you have chosen to follow a more rigid schedule to which your baby adheres, EC is probably not right for you. Strict schedules are typically designed by the parent and according to the parent's schedule, whereas EC requires the parent to follow the baby's lead.

It is also important to consider who else will be taking care of your child. Day cares cannot and will not participate in EC because it is against the law and licensing codes for a day care to have a consistently un-diapered baby on the premises. Likewise, EC requires one person to be alert to the baby's signals at all times, which is generally too difficult in a situation where one person is responsible for multiple infants in the same age range. This is not to say that a parent of multiple children cannot practice EC, but a parent of multiple infants may find this too difficult. EC becomes easier if some of the children are older, and thus more independent and capable of taking care of their own elimination needs.

One Mom's EC Story

"Years before I was a mom, I knew that I wanted to use EC with my children. When Thomas first showed signs, I snatched off his diaper and plopped him on his tiny potty. He immediately screamed, and my husband exclaimed "What are you doing to him?" An inauspicious start, but within two weeks, the crying subsided. For the next two months we had only a few dirty diapers, and I was with him constantly. Peeing proved to be more difficult to catch than pooping, but he and I were learning together and he was happy. He had a specific cry, and that meant we had around five minutes to find a bathroom. I quickly learned if I ignored his signal, he would grow increasingly upset until he was taken to eliminate.

"Soon, two things happened that made everything change. First, Thomas developed painful, frequent gas;

his response to gas was indistinguishable from his signal to poop. For two weeks we ran to the bathroom every few minutes, usually for nothing more than gas. Second, the worst cold snap hit Portland, turning our ill-sealed apartment into a fridge. When he was undressed to go to the toilet he shivered, looked at me in distress, and refused to pee or poop until he was redressed.

"By the time the cold snap finished, the combination of time away and continued gas had ruined our success. However, EC is based on communication, and so I continue to try. Even if I only occasionally catch elimination now, I still try to communicate anytime he signals. "Do you have gas?" "Do you have to poop?" "Are you going poop in your diaper?" "Good boy, going bathroom!" and change dirty diapers immediately. As a result, he still connects his body's signals with elimination. Sometimes we catch a poop or pee in the toilet, and sometimes Thomas startles his relatives by clearly asking for the bathroom at only thirteen months!"

–Jessica, mother to Thomas, age 13 months

Risks and Regression

As you probably noticed in Thomas's story, babies who are trained for EC can get very upset when they are not taken to eliminate. Just as potty-trained toddlers may cry or yell when they have an accident after they know they are supposed to wait for a toilet, babies who are used to using EC may grow confused, agitated, and even distressed by not using an elimination container or by not having someone respond quickly enough to their signals. This adds to the number of complications that accompany using EC.

At this point, you may ask yourself: what's the harm in trying? Well, if a baby is used to using a container with EC and his caregiver misses a signal or is unable to take him to the proper disposal container, he will often withhold his elimination. This means the infant is risking constipation, bowel compaction that can lead to bowel obstacles, urinary tract infections (UTI), and more.

✦ Essential

> Although many mothers have reported success using EC on a part-time basis, this may not work for everyone, and you as the parent will not have much choice about whether or not your baby is capable of part-time EC. Just as you cannot force a toddler to potty train before he is ready, you cannot force a baby to participate in EC.

Although these risks sound serious and can be serious, they are not exclusive to Elimination Communication. An infant using EC runs the risk of these consequences early in life if he doesn't have access to a container and has been trained not to eliminate in a diaper. On the other hand, a toddler who has not used EC is accustomed to eliminating in a diaper and will often withhold pee or poop when he is still getting used to a toilet. This, too, can cause constipation, bowel compaction, UTIs, and more. This section is not intended to frighten you or turn you on or off any one method of potty training. Instead, it is important that you familiarize yourself with the steps and potential consequences of each method as you determine which method is best for you.

The Pros and Cons of EC

As stated, EC is not for every parent or every child; it has both its rewards and risks. Here are a few of the pros and cons to consider as you explore Elimination Communication.

Pros and Cons of Elimination Communication

Pros	Cons
Encourages a deeper bond between parents and infants	Can be frustrating early on
Encourages early comprehension of some of the steps associated with potty training	Can be hard to determine signals from your baby
Reduces the mess associated with diapers	Can be hard to teach new signals to baby
Reduces the likelihood of diaper rashes	Cannot easily be done part-time
Reduces the amount of supplies needed in a diaper bag	Must be taught to anyone who will be caring for baby
Encourages communication to the parent early on	Cannot be done in a day care center
Encourages communication from the parent early on	May encounter regression much earlier than you would with potty training
Uses a centuries-old practice to maintain a hygienic practice in lieu of diapers	May confuse signals

Potty Training the EC Child

A lot of parents read about EC and wonder if this isn't really just potty training from the earliest possible age. Ingrid Bauer, author of *Diaper Free! The Gentle Wisdom of Natural Infant Hygiene*, explains that it is important to separate potty training from EC. She writes, "Toilet mastery is, of course, an inevitable consequence, yet it's no more the goal of Natural Infant Hygiene than weaning is the goal of breastfeeding." This means it is important not only to understand what you are accomplishing when you begin EC with your infant, but also to understand that you will still have potty training in front of you as your child achieves mobility. Many parents make the mistake of assuming an EC infant becomes a potty-trained child automatically. However, there are still many steps to transitioning your child from the parent-accompanied peeing or pooping that comes with EC, and the independent elimination that comes with being a successfully potty-trained child. Here are some steps to help the transition.

Step 1: Transition to the Appropriate Container

If you are using EC, chances are good that you have already started transitioning your child into sitting by herself by the time she approaches a reasonable potty-training age. You are likely carrying or accompanying your child to her elimination area, but you may still lift her onto her seat, help her with her clothing, and hold her at the beginning and ending of elimination. Now it's time to help her transition into independent potty time! Now would be a good time to make sure her elimination container is a reasonable place for a toddler to pee or poop by herself. You may have used a plastic container or bowl of your own determination for your early years of EC, but now it's time to switch to the potty chair or toilet you intend for your independent toddler to use. You will need to help your child make her transition from EC container to toilet just as a diaper-wearing toddler needs help making the transition from a diaper to a potty chair or toilet. Take baby steps toward your final goal, and give your child some time to get used to the new container before you begin the next step.

Step 2: Adjusting Her Own Clothes

Now that your toddler can identify the toilet or potty chair as the place where she goes to pee and poop, help her learn to raise and lower her own clothing. You can practice this goal when your child is getting ready for bed, getting up in the morning, and any other time she needs to change her clothes. This is another step that may have to be broken down into smaller steps before it's fully accomplished. Remember, a potty-trained child is one who can use the toilet completely on her own. In the past you have likely adjusted her clothing for her because you were likely holding her for most of the time she was eliminating. Now you'll be letting her do this for herself. Adjusting clothing on her own will also help you transition into the next step.

Step 3: Sitting by Herself

Depending on the toilet or potty chair you are using, it may be necessary for you to purchase a stepstool of some kind in order to help your child reach the height of her new elimination container. This step is one that proves hardest for children who practiced EC as infants because, up to this point, peeing and pooping has still been a bonding experience between you and your child. She has grown accustomed to the embracing, the interchange of sounds (or maybe words), and the intimacy of that moment with you. To become a potty-trained toddler, she must now want to be independent from you and relinquish this particular bonding experience. The job falls on you then to coach her about the joys of becoming a big kid, doing things by herself, and reaching the final goal of being a potty-trained toddler.

Your first step here is to get her accustomed to sitting on the toilet by herself. Prepare yourself; you may hear a variety of complaints here! Your toddler may worry about falling in, getting her hair in the water or waste, having a monster come out of the toilet, and more. Don't worry! This is all a normal part of the potty-training process. As a parent who has thus far practiced EC, you will more than likely avoid the concerns regarding the big empty space beneath her and the possibility of filling the container that other toddlers have. However, remember that EC is not potty training, and so you should be prepared for these concerns as they arise. Begin by helping your toddler sit on the toilet as she usually does with you beside her, but then leave her for small intervals as she eliminates. (It's best if you leave the room entirely in order to help her grow accustomed to your absence.)

Because you will be leaving the room completely, it is more important than ever now to make sure your toddler is ready for potty training. Every parent grows excited at some point about helping their child become independent in peeing and pooping, but your child's safety is still the most important element. Children as young as eighteen months can be physically strong enough and mentally prepared enough to hold themselves on a toilet seat, but as always, there is no definite age here. Watch your child in the beginning for strength, stability, and comprehension of what he is doing. Many toddlers get excited about this new height they have achieved and look at the toilet as a climbing tool to reach even higher. You must be sure your toddler is past this stage before you can safely leave him in the bathroom by herself.

After you have begun leaving him for brief intervals, you should also consider ways to make up for the lost bonding experience. Children who are not familiar with EC may adjust easier to sitting by themselves because they haven't lost an opportunity to bond with their parents, but children brought up with EC will likely look for a replacement time for bonding. Try adding a few moments in your day for quiet cuddling between you and your toddler to help replace the bathroom bonding and to alleviate his concerns regarding special time with Mommy or Daddy.

Step 4: Trying It on Her Own!

Once she has gotten used to adjusting her clothes, climbing on the toilet, and sitting by herself, your toddler is ready to try using the bathroom by herself. She is used to communicating with you about when she needs to go to the bathroom, and now all she needs is affirmation from you to use the bathroom parent-free. Now when you hear a signal from her that says she needs to go to the bathroom, encourage her to go by herself. Remind her that she knows how to follow all of the steps to eliminating by herself, and that you will be ready to cuddle her and applaud once she has peed or pooped on her own!

A Final Note on EC

Although Elimination Communication is not a common practice in the United States and is not endorsed by all pediatricians, it is still a clean, efficient way to begin forming a bond with your baby at an early age. Because of the many components of EC that are not part of a typical day, it's important to carefully consider all aspects of EC before you choose whether or not this is the best method for you. As with any child-rearing method, it is important not to punish yourself or your child if you feel you've made the wrong decision. If you choose not to use EC and then change your mind as your relationship with your child progresses, it's never too late to try using EC. By the same token, if you choose to use EC and realize the method is not compatible with your child-rearing methods or your relationship with your child, you don't have to continue. Choose the method that works best for you and feel confident in your decision. You are the parent, after all!

CHAPTER 4

The Fast Track: Potty Training in a Day or Two

One way to train children quickly is to utilize the parent-oriented method of potty training in only a day or two. Instead of gradually training your toddler over several weeks or months, many parents decide to jump in with both feet and accomplish the toilet training task in a condensed session, like over a weekend when other obligations will not inhibit their progress. Working parents find this to be the best time to concentrate on their toddler and provide consistent instruction. Although this method is often referred to by the harsh moniker of Baby Boot Camp, the fast track has been successful for many families.

About The Fast Track Method

The fast track potty-training method has been utilized by parents since the early 1970s. An early study of this method demonstrated that children between twenty and thirty-six months who had previously been difficult to train were completely trained within four hours of using the method. Likewise, there were few accidents reported in a four-month follow up. In the book, *Toilet Training in Less than a Day* (1974), authors Nathan H. Azrin and Richard M. Foxx describe this technique in further detail. This type of training has also been referred to as the Azrin and Foxx Method.

The fast track method uses positive reinforcement and rewards to teach the child toilet training habits without the need for reminders or assistance. These rewards usually come in the form of parental affection, toys, and candy. Despite its reported success, most pediatric health care providers do not recommend this method to patients. One reason for the lack of approval is the suggestion that children be given consequences for accidents, either through punishment or decreased positive attention. Other methods are more focused on positive reinforcement and omit any negative feedback.

Toilet training with the fast track method typically begins around the age of twenty months. All of the rules of readiness still apply. Is your child verbal? Does your child have bladder control? In other words, does he urinate all at once or is there a constant dribble of urine?

Does he stay dry for several hours? Does he seem to know when he is about to urinate (e.g., change in expression or change in stance)? Is he physically ready (i.e., is he able to pick things up easily and walk without help)? Can he follow simple instructions? To determine how well your child can follow instructions you can use the following tasks:

- Point to your nose
- Point to your eyes
- Point to your mouth
- Point to your hair
- Sit on the chair
- Stand up
- Walk with me to the kitchen (or other room)
- Cover your mouth
- Go and get your shoes
- Place this block inside this cup

If your child is able to accomplish each of these tasks, then he is ready to proceed with potty training.

Preparing for Success

In addition to assessing your toddler for readiness you may want to spend some time in "pretraining." During pretraining you will want to review and reinforce issues surrounding potty time. If your child has not previously helped in dressing and undressing herself, this is the time to help her learn. She will need to be able to raise and lower her pants without help. Remember, the goal of the fast track method is to teach your child to independently use the potty with little to no verbal cues or assistance from you.

Also during pretraining, it is recommended that you allow the child to watch others use the potty while you explain the steps the person is following. This person will likely be you, so be ready for any questions that may come up during a trip to the restroom. You may have the opportunity to explain topics such as pubic hair, tampons, and anatomy differences between boys and girls. Remember: do not reply with emotion. This may create curiosity in your child and prompt further questioning. Additionally, remember to reply in simple terms; sometimes your toddler just wants a one- or two-word answer. There is a great chance she will never ask again. Obviously this invasion of restroom privacy is not for every family. If you choose to skip this step, potty training can proceed as planned.

Pretraining is also an opportunity for you to identify and teach your toddler the words you will be using for urination, bowel movements, and body parts. See Chapter 2 for more detail.

Don't forget that you are working with a toddler, and that all toddlers are prone to mood swings. She will be happy and playful in one minute while the next minute brings a temper tantrum like no other. Do not let these tantrums discourage your progress; at this age, your role as the parent forces you to carefully choose your battles. Any battle you decide to choose *must* be won by you. You are the parent. You are not your child's friend or buddy. You are the authority in the home. If you fail to recognize and act on this, then you've put a two-year-old in charge of your home.

If you use the "time out" method to discipline your child, it is in your best interest to carefully consider clashes in your parenting philosophy before beginning this method of potty training. This parent-oriented approach to potty training comes from a different philosophy for resolving conflicts between parents and children. Instead of providing a time for your child to calm down following a problem, parents must be ready to confront uncooperative toddlers. This is difficult for parents who have little experience managing conflict in this way.

Parents must also recognize their own emotional limitations. Potty training, as with parenting in general, is not for the faint of heart. Parents must exercise self-control over their responses to the uncooperative toddler in order to avoid lashing out or abusive behaviors. Children who experience such negative reinforcement from parents and caregivers are at risk of serious setbacks, one of which may include a prolonged need for potty training. Setbacks may also manifest as frequent wetting and soiling of underwear. If either you or your partner is concerned about lashing out, do not continue training. Stop and regroup before working with your toddler again. The quest for a diaper-free toddler is worth far less than a solid, trusting, fear-free relationship between parents and their child.

Choose a Time

Now that you have assessed both your and your child's readiness, you need to select a time or date. It is in your best interest to select an entire weekend without any distractions. Place all other commitments on hold (no pun intended). One way to approach this is as an intense bonding between you and your toddler. You and your child will be together during every waking hour in order for you to assess her signals for bowel and bladder activity, so it is essential that you approach this process with a positive attitude. There should be no television or radio on the day of training. You may want to consider turning your phones off in order to avoid that interruption from the telemarketer or family member that causes you to miss your toddler's hurried trip to the potty and results in an accident. If you have older children, it is a good idea to make arrangements for them to be away from home to further prevent distractions for you and your toddler.

Even though the fast track method is viewed as a parent-oriented approach to potty training, there are several child-oriented factors to consider. One is choosing a time to potty train when your toddler is typically in a good mood. For example, if your toddler is teething and fussy, it is probably not advisable to introduce such a stringent concept; both of you will become frustrated far too early in the day. Reschedule for another weekend. Likewise, if you find yourself in the middle of your two-day intensive training regimen, but your toddler has decided she no longer wishes to play, stop the process and resume the next week.

Let your child know ahead of time what you will be doing the day before you begin the fast track method; she really needs no more notice than that. Tell her about your fun or special day that you have planned. It is not a bad idea to show her the cool new underpants she will get to wear. Remember to speak to her in terms she will understand. Phrases such as, "You will get to potty like Mommy," and, "You will get to wear big girl underwear," are motivating to the toddler who is looking for independence. Your excitement will be contagious, and she too will become energized and work to please you. She will want to show you her independence.

Be Prepared to be Patient

Remember, this method requires constant rewards for cooperation without punishment. This method is very strict, but being strict is very different than being angry. Be careful not to confuse discipline with anger. Consider the possibility that your protesting toddler may require redirection to the potty several times in a row. Patience is required as you gently, yet decisively, help her sit down again and again. Show your toddler that you can handle her with ease, thereby demonstrating discipline, not anger or frustration. Give positive feedback for the smallest of victories by saying, for example, "Look at the great job you are doing sitting here! I am very proud of you." You may need to call on your best acting talent to encourage your toddler. Pretend as though you think she misunderstood the directive. It is quite possible that you know she clearly understood your request, yet she disobeyed because her actions were based in stubbornness.

Supplies for Boot Camp

Be sure to gather all of the supplies you will need before you begin training. It is very disappointing to eager parents to begin the process and then be forced to stop abruptly when they run out of something. Here is a suggested list of supplies for your weekend's work:

List of Supplies

Supply (Quantity)	Purpose
Doll that wets with bottle and underpants (1)	This is a great way to demonstrate the process of drinking followed by wetting.
Drinks (Several)	Choose your child's favorite beverages. Be sure to get a variety, as his preference may change throughout the day. Frequent liquid intake is important to ensure frequent trips to the potty. Buy more than you think you will need; the drinks will not go to waste.
Salty snacks (Several)	Pretzels, potato chips, and crackers. This may be counter to your typical dietary intake, but remember that it's only for two days. The saltiness of these snacks will make your toddler thirsty. As with the drinks, buy more than you think you will need; you can use them for special treats later.

Supply (Quantity)	Purpose
Panties or Underwear (eight pairs, at least)	It is better to use cloth panties instead of disposable briefs for boot camp. Cloth panties help you immediately realize when your child becomes wet or soiled. It is recommended that these panties be 2–3 sizes larger than normal to facilitate easier removal at the potty.
Potty chair or potty seat (1)	Some parents prefer to use a chair that signals (lights up, plays music, etc.) when it is wet. This is not necessary but may be useful.
Stepstool (1)	If you are using an adult potty with a potty seat, the step stool ensures the proper positioning of your toddler's legs for bowel movements. In addition, it can be used to help him reach the sink when washing his hands after using the potty.
List of favorite people and characters (One list, several people)	Having a list of admired characters or people is useful for praising your child and letting him know how pleased they will be when they hear of his success.
Loose clothing (short T-shirt, elasticized pants or shorts, three to four changes of clothes)	Baggier clothes will prevent interference when your child rushes to the bathroom.

Step 1: Practice with a Doll

Playing with dolls or babies is not something boys typically have the opportunity to do. Girls, however, are usually naturals with babies and pretend play. You may need to use your imagination when attempting to engage your son in pretend play. You may need to engage him in naming the doll or deciding it looks like a friend's baby in order to help him work with the doll. To begin, have your child dress the doll with its underwear. Fill the doll bottle with water and allow your child to feed it. Show your child how the doll now needs to urinate and talk him through the steps of going to the potty. You may want to say something like, "It is time to take the doll to the potty. Take off her pants. Help her sit on the potty. Now watch between her legs." To adults, these are the boring details of going to the restroom. To your toddler, this is amazing stuff. Now make the doll release the water and get the attention of your toddler. Show your toddler how to reward the doll's behavior with praise and a pretend snack or drink. These are important details since his good behavior will be rewarded much the same way.

If you are using a potty chair, show your toddler how to remove the receptacle, pour the contents into the toilet bowl, flush the toilet, rinse the receptacle, and replace it in the potty. Your toddler needs continuous praise and reinforcement. If you tend to be the type of person who is a word miser, you will need to step outside your comfort zone and become more verbose. He needs praise for even the tiniest accomplishment.

Once you have praised your toddler for his accomplishments, it's back to work. You will have your toddler replace the doll's underwear. This is a good time to teach him to check his own underwear to see if it are wet or dry. You can encourage this by teaching him to check the underwear of his doll. When he correctly identifies whether or not the doll's pants are dry, reward him with something to drink. Now show him how to check his own pants for wetness. Each time he correctly identifies wet and dry, offer a reward of juice or snacks. Remember to over-emphasize each piece of verbal praise you give him.

⊖❗ Alert

> Training Tip: During boot camp, follow your toddler's normal nap and meal pattern. This prevents the problems brought on by having a grumpy child during the day. Put your toddler in a diaper or disposable brief during napping and bedtime. The fast track method is for daytime dryness only.

Now it is time to test your toddler to find out what he has he learned so far. When he is distracted, pour a small amount of water on the underpants of the doll. Ask him to check its pants again for dryness. When he tells you the doll's pants are wet, talk to him about accidents. Change the tone of your voice to become stern. Use phrases like, "Oh no! Big boys do not wet their pants," or "It is not okay to wet our pants." Then instruct your toddler that he will need to help the doll practice going to the potty so that it will no longer have accidents.

If your temperament is such that you hate repeating yourself, this part of potty boot camp will become really old really fast. Not only will you have your toddler practice with the doll several times after an accident, but you will also have your toddler do the same after any accident he may have during the day. Have him take the doll back and forth between the potty and where the doll wet its pants. Have him place the doll briefly on the potty then return to the accident. Help him understand that, like his doll, he must hurry to the potty so that he will stay dry and avoid accidents. Now, when it comes to your toddler practicing after a wet accident, he will likely become annoyed with this repetition of running between the potty and the scene of the accident. Be prepared for a struggle, and remember to exercise restraint as you both become frustrated. Remember to continue to offer drinks frequently as reward for adhering to the process.

Don't forget how important your reactions are to your toddler during this process. He needs to know that you are supportive yet stern. Kind words and encouragement are essential to his ability to achieve a sense of independence and success. You will use several different phrases to affirm your child's progress. Remember the list of other people who use the potty you constructed? This is where you use the names on the list as clout. "Daddy uses a big boy potty. Are you going to use the big boy potty?" "Diego uses a big boy potty, too. He will be very proud of you." Throughout the day you will probably use your "A" list people and dip into the "B" list as well. Your toddler will not notice if you use someone more than once during the day.

Step 2: Practice with the Potty

Now it is time to have your toddler practice getting to the potty chair herself. You will show her how to get to the chair, pull down her pants, sit down, and, after a few minutes, get up, pull her pants back up, and move away. Urination on the first or second try may come as a surprise to you and your toddler. Little girls especially need to be watched closely when sitting so that you can see urination begin. Praise, praise, and more praise should be given when your toddler pees in the potty. Likely she has urinated because you have offered many liquid refreshments to this point. Your toddler needs lots of smiles, hugs, and kind words, especially because she has done something new today. Don't forget her reward of salty snacks and drinks.

 Alert

A tantrum while on the potty is counterproductive. Do not let an upset toddler or highly tempered infant remain seated on the potty chair for more than a few minutes. It will not facilitate her ability to relax and urinate if she is battling her own frustration.

If your toddler did not urinate immediately, have her stay on the potty for at least ten minutes. Rowdy toddlers will not enjoy this eternity of sitting, so you must use all of your tricks to coax her into staying put. If she refuses, you must use stern language and gentle pressure to reposition her on the potty. This repetition is necessary only until the first time she urinates in the potty. Each time after that requires she sit on the potty for five minutes. Wiggling and restlessness are to be expected from every toddler during potty time. Try to help her relax while she is on the potty by talking, singing, or reading to her.

Relaxation on the potty is key to the success of potty training. Your child will take much needed breaks between sitting sessions. Give her ten minutes of rest and then back to work she goes. Remember to reward all positive behaviors with drinks and snacks and use words of encouragement when she stays seated for several minutes in a row. This keeps the cycle of urination going.

It is important to utilize the break time in boot camp. Your child needs breaks so that she can begin to recognize the sensations associated with urination. While she is on a break, allow her to read books and play with the doll. This gives further opportunity for reinforcement of the teaching you have done thus far. If an accident occurs during break time, reassure your toddler that you are teaching her about getting to the potty in time. There is *no* punishment for an accident, but you may use stern language to dissuade a repeat of this behavior. Withhold rewards when your child has an accident or fails to carry out your request during the training process. If your child has an accident, begin the practice procedure again (getting to the potty, lowering pants, sitting for a few seconds, then raising pants and returning to the area where the accident occurred). There is no need to have her sit for an extended period since this will only increase the frustration on both your parts.

Remember that the main goal of fast track potty training is to teach the toddler how to become fully independent in self-toileting, so an objective of your practice time is to get your child to go to the potty without being told to do so. When she struggles with the choices of going to the potty versus staying put, use verbal feedback to encourage her to comply. If she continues to be reluctant to go to the potty, help her by gently leading her to the potty and helping her to get seated. This may require several attempts during practice. Again, encourage her with kind words; "Look at you! You are going to the potty. Grammy will be so proud of you." Sometimes, the positive affirmations are for you as much as they are for your toddler.

Potty-Training Boot Camp was started by using very direct commands to your toddler to get her to the potty successfully. Once she has mastered the ability to get to the potty, it is time to revise the commands. Instead of, "Go to the potty," you will say something like, "Would you like to go to the potty?" There is a good chance your little darling will give you an emphatic, "NO!" If she chooses not to go to the potty with the gentler directive, return to the stern command. Not going to the potty is not an option for her at this time. If necessary, you will again gently guide her to the potty chair using gentle pressure. Repeat this process as long as necessary until she is able to walk to the potty, lower her pants, sit down, and potty. Teach your child to empty the receptacle following urination and to replace it, too. Mastering even the simplest tasks can give your child extreme satisfaction.

Handling Tantrums

Tantrums may be sparse or abundant, depending on your child's mood on the day of potty-training boot camp. Help your child get through the tantrums by keeping a calm, cool demeanor and offering frequent reassurance to your child during tantrums. Let her know she will be successful soon. Tantrums should not, however, be used as an excuse to abandon boot camp. You are the one in control of this process, not your toddler. Maintain your emotional integrity and press on.

After several hours of boot camp, your toddler may become tired, increasing the likelihood of tantrums. If she is inconsolable, stop practicing until she calms down; you can resume practice when she is ready. Let her have more juice and snacks once she is calm. Resume practice at the point where you stopped prior to the tantrum, thereby demonstrating to your toddler that she still must carry out the behavior you expect. Her tantrum did not exempt her from obedience.

Usually after the third tantrum the toddler settles in and decides to become more compliant with toileting activities. As soon as you notice your toddler heading to the potty without prompting, shower her with praise and encouragement. Over-emphasize your pleasure, and she will likely respond by striving to do the same thing again.

Accidents During Boot Camp

If you have had good luck so far, congratulations! Get ready, though, because your toddler will likely have an accident at some point during boot camp. Since the goal of the fast track method is total independence of the child, your commands for getting her to the potty have become gentle to the point of silence at this point. Since you may no longer be offering those verbal cues, at some point she will more than likely get to the potty too late or perhaps not attempt to get there at all. It is quite possible that she does not realize that this game you two have been playing all day is part of a permanent change in her routine.

The fast track method demands strict, stern commands during the training period. It also demands stern reprimands for accidents, but this does not mean you should yell at your child. You should, for example, use a stronger tone to your voice when you say, "No! Do not wet your pants." For some children, this verbal warning is enough. Your toddler may cry and have hurt feelings because of the change in your voice. She does not want to disappoint you.

Following an accident, it is important to have your toddler change her own wet or soiled underwear. She must become used to the process of taking dirty ones off, cleaning her bottom, and putting on clean underpants. Keep your expectations realistic, though. You should not expect her to independently clean herself after bowel movements just yet. Even school age children require help for this task from time to time. After she is clean, review the steps of checking for wet and dry underwear. Have her touch her hand to the crotch of the underpants to check for dryness. If she tells you she is dry correctly, offer juice and a snack as a reward. Next, have her practice getting to the potty quickly, pulling down her underpants, sitting on the potty, standing and pulling up her underpants, and returning to the site of the accident. This practice and repetition of steps helps your child understand the importance of getting to the potty when she first feels the urge to go.

Have her help you clean up after her accident. Be sure to remind her that wet pants are not okay. Use language like, "Mommy does not like it when you wet your pants."

Watch Your Tone

Since you have embarked on this parent-oriented style of potty training, you are probably at least somewhat comfortable with using stern tones and confronting unacceptable behaviors like accidents. However, even at this point, some parents may still be bargaining with their toddlers to do the right thing. Do not commit the fatal error of whining at your toddler. How many times have you heard a parent say something like, "Do not do thaaaaaat, please?" or "Sweetie, you will make Mommy cryyyyy." Notice the direct, firm statement in the previous paragraph; there is no room for discussion there. Your toddler needs boundaries and security. She needs to know that you are in charge in every situation. Otherwise, she senses instability in her surroundings and her foundation for learning is faulty. She is counting on you to provide guidance and you are no longer guiding her once the whining begins. Instead, you've lowered yourself to her level of development. If a choice is realistically an option, you may offer it, but don't give choices in situations where one does not exist. For example, in boot camp your toddler may choose the salty snack she wants as a reward, but she may not have a choice of whether or not she will sit on the potty. If giving direct commands feels uncomfortable to you, you may choose to use a more child-oriented method of potty training. A second option would be to practice using this direct approach in other aspects of parenting and resuming the fast track method at a later time.

When You Just Can't Go On

Maybe you picked the wrong day. Maybe your toddler is coming down with a cold. Maybe he didn't sleep well the night before. Whatever the case may be, exhaustion of the child is a valid reason to put boot camp on hold. Don't worry; your time investment has not gone entirely to waste. For the rest of the day and for the next several days, you will continue to do the elimination related work for your child. Do not place any more demands on him, simply because it will be frustrating for both of you. Check his pants on waking, after naps, and before meals or snacks. Praise him when he is dry, and continue to take him to the potty from time to time, especially if it looks like he needs to use it. Instead of having him clean up after an accident, you will clean him. Don't revert to diapers during the day, but rather keep him in underwear. Cover him with waterproof pants if he continues to have accidents. At this point it is also recommended to continue using diapers or disposable briefs for naps and overnight for children younger than thirty months. If your child is over thirty months, use panties or underwear for naps and over-night. Make sure these are easy to pull on and off for nighttime trips to the potty. You will want to protect his bed with a waterproof sheet that can be easily removed during those middle-of-the-night linen changes.

Going to the Potty at Night

Now that your child is becoming more aware of the sensations associated with going to the potty, she may wake at night for a trip to urinate. Make sure you have the bathroom ready to go, and use nightlights for the hallway and bathroom. It may be scary for the toddler walking into a darkened bathroom at night. Don't be surprised if your toddler passes two bathrooms only to come into your room to let you know she needs to potty. Help her get to the bathroom and promptly return to bed. She may need a little extra help at night for a short time. Gently remind her that her bathroom has a light and is ready for her, but do not reprimand her for coming to you. She is still making great progress.

The nighttime wake-up is often an after-the-fact event in the first few weeks of potty training meaning that your toddler has already had an accident. In that case, you have options. You may wish to do a complete linen change and put her back to bed afterward. You may decide to remove the wet linens and place temporary bedding so that both of you can get back to sleep quickly, or you may want to have a sleeping bag handy and have your toddler finish the night there. Only you know the option your toddler will comply with best.

The Home Stretch

Now you and your toddler are approaching the end of the fast track potty-training method. Your one- to two-day intensive boot camp is almost over. What next? Your toddler has mastered getting to the potty, and accidents are at a minimum. Even after he has been fairly consistent in using the potty, you will continue to check his underwear throughout the day for dryness. Repetition is the key to success, so offer drinks and salty snacks all day to promote frequent trips to the potty.

You will know your work is complete when your toddler is able to get to the potty on his own and complete all of the potty-training tasks discussed in this chapter without your prompting or assistance. After giving your toddler lots of praise throughout the day for his good choices and work, it's now time to give only a smile for using the potty. Continue to work with your toddler after accidents and use those stern reprimands to convey your message. Being consistent is important as you help him correct his mistakes or accidents. Once he has had two completely dry days (not nights), it is time to consider your toddler fully potty trained. Celebrate his success. In fact, celebrate your success, too. This is an accomplishment you both should be proud of.

Summary of Steps for the Fast Track Method

- Use a doll that wets to teach your toddler the process of going to the potty. Guide your child through the proper actions first, and then have your child guide the doll through the actions without you.
- Once the doll urinates in the potty, teach your child how to empty the receptacle into the toilet, flush the toilet, and replace the receptacle in the potty chair.
- Teach the child to check for dry pants versus wet pants. Reward and praise her for correct identification. Check her every three to five minutes for wetness. You may want to use a notebook to remind you of the time of your last inspection.
- Give your toddler as much to drink as you can (suggestion: eight ounces every hour). This much fluid will result in frequent trips to the potty, creating more practice opportunities. Use positive reinforcement (drinks and salty snacks) after successful urination or bowel movements.
- Instruct your child to go to the potty, pull down her pants, sit down quietly for ten minutes, stand up, and pull up her pants. If urination occurs, reward with hugs, drinks, and salty snacks.

- Conduct "potty practice" every fifteen minutes at the beginning of the day. Decrease the frequency as she achieves more success.
- Check for dry pants every five minutes. Your child should also check.
- After two or three successful trips of sitting on the potty for ten minutes, you can reduce the number of minutes your child sits to five.
- Gradually change your directions from "Go to the potty" to asking your child if she needs to potty. You may use questions like "Where do you go potty?" Once she has gone to the potty, comment only on dry pants.
- Give positive affirmation during the steps early in the day. As your child success rate increases, restrict your comments to only after completion of a task. As the process goes on, reduce your comments further to include only praise for staying dry.
- Conduct dry pants checks for several days following boot camp. Check pants after naps and bedtime and before snacks and meals. Praise each time there are dry pants.
- Reprimand for accidents. Have your toddler change the wet pants by herself. Resume practice sessions after any accident. You will no longer give reminders to potty.

The Pros and Cons of the Fast Track Method

Pros

- Quick
- Simple concept
- Excellent resources
- Great for more developmental mature toddlers
- Great for parents who use a more authoritative style of parenting

Cons

- Requires full focus of parental attention for the length of training (one to two days)
- Pretraining is not avoidable
- Difficult to use with younger toddlers
- Difficult to use for parents who prefer a more permissive style of parenting
- May need to abandon plans if child becomes ill or excessively irritable

CHAPTER 5

The Slow and Steady Approach to Potty Training

Introduced by Dr. T. Berry Brazelton in 1962, the child-oriented approach to potty training has long been a favorite of pediatric health care providers and has been well-discussed in pediatric literature for more than thirty-five years. Unlike the parent-oriented approach, this method emphasizes a gradual approach that should only begin after your toddler has achieved certain physical and psychological milestones. The parent and the child both participate in the process. Despite the lack of published information regarding outcomes, the Brazelton method remains a favorite among parents and providers.

Child-Oriented Approach

Brazelton's method is a true, child-oriented approach to potty training. He advocates that the toddler show true signs of readiness prior to beginning the process (able to follow commands, uses two word phrases, walks with ease, etc.) For a complete list of the signs of readiness, see Chapter 1. Brazelton's method does not assign a specific age to begin the process, although many of the readiness signs should be visible by about eighteen months of age. Brazelton is a strong supporter of using positive words to praise your toddler. He further recommends that no punishment, shaming, or force be used when potty training toddlers. The Brazelton method emphasizes a natural approach that keeps potty training positive and stress free.

The idea of a child-oriented approach is not new. As early as the 1940s, Dr. Benjamin Spock recommended that parents train without forcing their youngster into submission. He, like Brazelton, emphasized the importance of identifying the readiness of the child before embarking on the potty-training process. Dr. Spock recommended all training begin sometime between twenty-four and thirty months of age. He supported the notion that children should be allowed to accompany family members to the potty as often as possible. Dr. Spock also discussed the importance of creating a stress-free process for potty training. He believed parents should avoid criticizing their toddlers as well as any negative comments about bowel movements (e.g. "Shoo-wee. That is smelly."). In addition, Dr. Spock's method called for the child to be allowed to use his potty chair only if he wanted to use it. Taking him to the potty should only be done routinely after he shows interest in sitting on it voluntarily. Like Brazelton, Dr. Spock recognized the vital role frequent praise played in the toddler's success.

ⓔ✔ Fact

Dr. Benjamin Spock was an American pediatrician who published his bestselling book, *Baby and Child Care*, in 1946. Dr. Spock used psychoanalysis to gain a better understanding of children. He encouraged more patience and understanding from parents, along with increased affection and bonding between parents and children. He emphasized that children are also individuals who require tolerance over discipline, and need to be treated as individuals in order to better benefit from childhood experiences and parenting methods.

In 2000, the American Academy of Pediatrics (AAP) developed guidelines for potty training using several components of the previous child-oriented approaches. The AAP recommendations are similar to those of Brazelton in that toddlers should not be forced into potty training on the parent's schedule but rather be allowed to progress at their own pace. Children should begin potty training only when they are ready from a behavioral, emotional, and developmental standpoint. Like the Brazelton method, the AAP feels that potty training should begin sometime after the eighteenth month of life but closer to the age of three years. In fact, about one-third of toddlers are still in diapers beyond their third birthday. One difference between the two potty-training programs is that the AAP recommends parents reward children with praise and positive reinforcement instead of treats.

But you may ask, what about all of the stories you have heard from your mother and grandmother about how all their kids were trained by the time they were eighteen months old? Part of the reason this may actually be true is due to the pre-Brazelton and Spock philosophy of parents and health care providers. Prior to the eighteenth century, infants were mostly left without diapers and encouraged to go potty outside. Since indoor plumbing was not available and disposable diapers had not been invented, this drastically reduced the amount of laundry for that generation's moms. When the eighteenth century rolled in, so did indoor facilities. Families began to encourage children to potty train, and thus the battle of wills between toddlers and parents was born. Parents trained infants to use the potty as early as three months of age in the 1930s with claims that healthy babies could be completely trained by eight months (See Chapter 3 for more information).

Drs. Spock and Brazelton were able to convince the world that forcing children to use the potty before they are ready has potentially negative outcomes. Spock and Brazelton believed that rushed and rigid methods are usually unsuccessful and created an environment where behavioral and emotional problems flourish. Conversely, those who subscribe to the fast track method discussed in Chapter 4 argue that the parent-oriented approach is what is necessary to correct the coddled, self-entitled, and spoiled youth of this generation. The AAP adopted many of the components of the methods of Spock and Brazelton to further develop a potty-training program that recognizes parental readiness and builds the self-esteem of the toddler as he masters this developmental milestone.

Now that you have evaluated the difference between parent- and child-oriented approaches to potty training, you must decide which method works best for you and your little one. Is there truly a right way and a wrong way? Only if the approach you choose does not match the needs of your family. Be assured that deciding to abandon one method to begin a different method will not cause your child a lifetime of psychoanalysis. The over-riding theme for any method you choose is that there is no room for punishment or demeaning behavior in any way. Potty training is not a competition between toddler and parent, nor should it hurt your relationship with him. Remember, *you* are the parent. *You* are the decision maker. *You* set the tone for successful potty training. Keep a sense of humor. You will need it.

Beginning the Process

Much like the parent-oriented approach in Chapter 4, your basic equipment is a potty chair or seat and optional snacks or treats. Since you will not be completing this in a single day or weekend, you do not need to over-purchase snacks, drinks, or underwear. The child-oriented method is a far more laid back approach and enlists the assistance of parents, grandparents, day care providers, and babysitters. One drawback is that parents will likely deal with accidents for an extended period of time and will be buying diapers or disposable briefs and wipes for a little longer. If you determine that you will have your potty-training tyke wear underwear, be prepared for increased laundry, hygiene challenges, and stains on carpeting and furniture. The practice of returning your toddler to diapers after several days of accidents has caused some concern over how this affects her self-esteem. In order to avoid this, consider either using disposable briefs or panties with a waterproof cover until she is accident-free for an extended period of time.

Once you have identified the readiness of your toddler, it is time to introduce the potty chair or potty seat. It is a good idea to take your toddler with you when you choose the potty accessory. In addition, let your toddler choose the underwear she would like to wear when she graduates to big girl pants. If your child has been following you or other family members to the bathroom, encourage her to sit on the new potty chair (fully clothed at first). Although keeping the potty chair in the restroom is strongly advised, it is not a requirement. In fact, if your toddler wants to sit on the potty chair to eat a snack at this point, it is okay. Don't require her to remain seated for an extended period of time; allow her to get up and down at will. While your child is seated, read her a story or talk to her to create a calm atmosphere in which she can associate a sense of comfort instead of stress.

After one to two weeks of having your toddler sit on the potty with all of her clothes on, ask her if she would like to try sitting on the chair without her diaper. Do not force her; remove her diaper only if she agrees with you. For now, do not require your child to actually use the potty. While you are preparing your toddler for the potty, encourage her by telling her that this is how Mommy and Daddy potty too. Once she is seated on her potty, you sit on the toilet. Your demonstration helps peak your child's natural instinct to act like you. She will attempt to mimic your behavior. Remember, if she is successful and urinates while practicing, you should give her lots of praise and positive reinforcement.

What's Next?

Your child is still in diapers at this point. After about one week of demonstrating sitting on the potty, take your child into the bathroom to change her soiled diaper. Remove the soiled diaper and empty the stool into the chair. While you are emptying the stool, explain what you are doing and why. Let her know that this is where stool goes. You will also demonstrate emptying the stool from the chair's receptacle into the toilet. Many toddlers will be fascinated by the sounds of the stool dropping into the toilet and the flush. Be aware that some toddlers will be scared by the flush of the commode. For this reason, you may find it best to allow your toddler to leave the bathroom before you flush. Explain to her that mommies and daddies use a toilet every day and their stool gets flushed away also. If your toddler is eager to help, allow her to do so. She may want to dump the stool into the toilet or flush the commode. This is a great way to engage her further in the potty-training process.

Potential Barriers

There are several obstacles that can affect the success of potty training in your toddler. One potential impediment is a urinary tract infection. Urinary tract infections (UTI) or bladder infections are more common in girls than boys. (Circumcision reduces the risk of a urinary tract infection in boys.) Children may develop a UTI when the bladder is unable to completely empty, as is often the case with constipation. Another cause of UTI is poor hygiene. The potty-training toddler is just becoming comfortable with the mechanics of wiping and may have problems getting completely clean after bowel movements. To avoid these problems, many pediatricians recommend that parents and caregivers assist in ensuring cleanliness following bowel movements. Symptoms of UTIs are increased frequency of urinations, urgency (very little notice between recognizing the need to go and going), painful urination, and, in more severe infections, fever and vomiting. Urine may have a strong, foul odor and look cloudy. The toddler with a UTI may also have a sudden increase in accidents. UTIs are typically ascending infections, meaning the infection starts nearer the urethra (opening for urination) and advances upward toward the bladder, ureters, and kidneys. If you are concerned about a UTI in your toddler, seek the help of your health care provider.

Constipation is another potential barrier to potty training. Researchers have noted that constipation occurs in approximately 80 percent of children who were difficult to potty train, whereas it was reported in only about 50 percent of children who potty trained without problems. Additionally, there are some toddlers who refuse to have a bowel movement in the potty in total. This concept is referred to as stool toileting refusal. Researchers and pediatricians estimate that slightly more than 50 percent of the children with stool toileting refusal are constipated. This creates a vicious cycle in your toddler.

PAMELA, mother to Emmit, 4, James, 3, and Brent, 6 months:

"When trying to potty train my oldest son, I used targets in the toilet to help him learn how to pee standing up and he was potty trained inside a week. When it came to pooping, however, he had the most unbelievable irrational fear I have ever seen. I tried to push the issue, but he absolutely refused to poop! As a result, he soon became extremely constipated. We endured three months of sitting with him on the toilet for an hour at a time while he screamed. At first we thought he was just throwing a tantrum out of stubbornness, but our doctor explained that he was actually constipated and the screams were because he was in pain!"

Even if your toddler has a bowel movement in his diaper every day, he still may be constipated. Toddlers are well known for being a constipated group. Constipation is technically defined as having fewer than three hard bowel movements per week. In children, however, bowel movements may be occurring daily yet in small, hard pellets instead of long, smooth "cigars." This hard consistency and small volume still equals constipation.

Help for Constipation

Constipation is best managed through dietary efforts. Unfortunately, as you are already aware, the toddler diet is fairly unreliable when it comes to taking in enough fiber and water each day. Theirs is a diet high in carbohydrates (crackers, pasta, etc.) and milk, all of which are notorious causes of constipation. Milk is frequently offered in volumes greater than necessary so that parents feel they can overcome the lack of nutrient intake in other food groups. A diet high in fiber is desired in order to combat constipation, but getting five to eight servings of fruits (except bananas) and vegetables into an active and picky two-year old is virtually impossible. As the parent, you must try to be creative in finding alternate methods of improving fiber intake. There are several items on the market to increase fiber including gummy fiber vitamins, fiber cookies, fiber bars, high fiber cereals, yogurt, and fiber snack mixes. Even toaster pastries are marketed as "high in fiber." Adding any of these to your child's nutrient intake will help naturally soften stool.

In some cases, dietary measures are not enough, and aggressive measures are warranted to facilitate bowel movements. When constipation is left untreated it can lead to painful bowel movements, so softening the stool is critical. Countless past examples of constipated children have proven that it takes only one painful episode of stooling to cause a child to withhold stool. This can become a vicious cycle that makes constipation worse. Prolonged constipation creates problems within the colon and rectum. These areas stretch, allowing softer stool to seep around the hard stool and causing soiling. This condition is called encopresis. Children with encopresis are unaware that they are passing soft stool but are often punished as parents feel that they have soiled their pants on purpose. Not only are these children embarrassed by the accident, but they are also often teased by their classmates and chastised by adults. If your toddler is experiencing severe constipation or encopresis, seek the clinical advice of your pediatric healthcare provider.

The Next Step

Now that you are able to identify potential deterrents to successful potty training, it is time to take the child-oriented approach to the next step. She has watched you go potty and has allowed you to help her sit on the potty. She may have even urinated or had a bowel movement at this point. It's now time to start taking your toddler to the toilet several times each day. As she becomes more comfortable and confident using the potty chair, remove the diaper for short intervals. Keep the potty chair handy so that she can use it independently throughout the day. In this method, gentle reminders from you are necessary to encourage her to go to the potty. If she is having success (few to no accidents), you may want to extend the amount of time she spends without a diaper if you have not already removed it. If she has an accident, reassure her. Accidents happen! Let her know that she may not quite be ready and place her back in disposable briefs.

It is at this point that many parents face a true battle of wills with their potty-training toddler. In some cases, the toddler refuses to wear the diaper or training pants, instead opting for underwear. However, she also refuses to use the potty. What is a parent to do? Likely she is experiencing an internal battle that is creating stress. Remember "Autonomy versus Shame and Doubt?" This goes back to the developmental task of your toddler. She must successfully transition to independence with potty training in order to escape shame from peers and self-doubt. That potty chair represents her next step toward being a big girl, but being a big girl means she is no longer the baby. Do not push your child in one direction over another; she will solve this portion of the dilemma herself. If you push too hard, the battle is likely to continue.

Once your little one has mastered these steps, move her into panties if you have not already done so. It is advisable to use underwear that is a couple of sizes too big so that she can pull them up and down independently. You may chose to use disposable training pants for a little while longer, and this is okay too. Remember, she's never done this before so she has no idea what the books say.

Some parents report their toddler did really well up to this point. She went to the potty—both urine and stool—without problems. Unfortunately, she lost interest in going to the potty after consistently using it for a few weeks. Many will associate the timing of such an event with a trip to Grandma's or changing classes at day care or something of the sort. These children suddenly decide that they would rather stay in their disposable briefs instead of dealing with accidents in underwear all day. Some just don't want to be bothered with the interruption created by making a trip to the potty.

In most instances, this is not an act of toddler defiance but rather is truly a situation where she faces her own dilemma. This toddler does not want to leave the home living center and lose her turn to go spend time in the bathroom alone. She would rather have an accident while staying to play until her time is up in the center. Some toddlers struggle with the notion that they are growing up and resist it until the bitter end. Do not be discouraged or angry; she will not be wearing diapers to college. If you see this resistance in your toddler, talk to her. Include her in discussions with both parents to determine if she should continue to wear disposable briefs or diapers until the accidents are gone.

Nighttime Dryness

Daytime dryness is achieved long before nighttime dryness in most cases. Often, toddlers are using the potty exclusively throughout the day with no accidents but continue to have accidents at night. It is quite likely that your toddler is sleeping too soundly to recognize the need to go to the bathroom. It's also possible that he feels the urge but does not want to get out of bed. The Brazelton method suggests that parents not wake children to take them to the potty during the night. He believes that this is another form of stress or pressure placed on the child and discourages parents from doing so. In the child-oriented approach, it's recommended that parents observe children for dryness during the day to determine nighttime capabilities. If your toddler is able to stay dry for four to six hours at a time during the day, try allowing him to sleep in big boy underwear at night. If he is not ready, don't fret; eventually he'll be ready. Often it is peer pressure that forces the issue; if your child's friends are showing off their new big boy underwear, he may be more likely to work on nighttime dryness.

 Fact

Many experts report that 15 percent of children are still bedwetting at age five. This number decreases to 7–10 percent by age seven. At age ten, about 3 percent boys and 2 percent of girls are still wetting the bed. By age eighteen only 1 percent of boys are having nighttime accidents.

This brings up the discussion regarding long term bedwetting. Daytime dryness is often achieved before nighttime dryness. In most children, nighttime dryness is achieved by three to four years. The average child may not stop having nighttime accidents until he is four or five years old, and it is still a common problem for six-to eight-year-olds. In fact, nocturnal enuresis (bedwetting) affects almost 8 percent of eight-year-olds. The number of children in the United States who are affected by bedwetting is approximately 5 to 7 million, numbers that should give most parents a little reassurance. Boys tend to have more problems than girls. Often children who are bedwetters have parents who were bedwetters.

The reasons for bedwetting are not well understood. Several different factors may contribute to bedwetting, including genetics, a small bladder capacity, stress, and an inability to recognize when the bladder is full. If both parents were bedwetters, there is a 77 percent chance that their child will be a bedwetter. This is reduced to 44 percent if just one parent was a bedwetter. If neither parent wet the bed as a child, the child still has about a 15 percent chance of having nighttime accidents. Having a small bladder capacity is another factor that may influence nighttime accidents. If a child's bladder cannot hold as much urine as his peers', or if there is a lack of the hormone vasopressin (helps regulate production of urine at night), nighttime dryness is delayed.

One other factor thought to contribute to nocturnal enuresis is an inability to recognize when the bladder is full. In other words, the child is a really deep sleeper and has difficulty rousing himself when the bladder attempts to signal that it is ready to be relieved.

Steps to Help Your Child Control Bedwetting

Until your child is able to reach maturity (this age is different for each child) and basically outgrow nocturnal enuresis, here are a few steps you can take to help increase the number of dry nights at your house:

- Reassure him that this is normal at his age and is not his fault. Make sure he knows you understand he is not wetting the bed on purpose.
- Do not punish him or blame him for wetting the bed. Do not allow other family members to tease him about wetting the bed.
- Avoid allowing your child to drink large amounts of fluid for the two hours just prior to bed time. (There is debate over whether or not this fluid restriction is effective).
- Always have him use the potty as the last thing he does before hopping into bed.
- Protect the mattress with a waterproof layer or mattress pad.
- Allow him to help change the wet linens after an accident. This creates a matter-of-fact environment so he can better realize accidents happen.
- Consider helping your child with bladder stretching exercises. Encourage him to increase the amount of time between urination during the daytime and increase this time in small increments. This may help the bladder hold more urine at night.
- Practice an awakening routine. Wake your child approximately two to three hours after he goes to bed and help him to the potty. You may wish to do this when you go to bed or you may want to set an alarm to wake him.

- Avoid caffeinated drinks. Caffeine is a bladder irritant.
- Use disposable briefs until your child is able to experience several dry nights in a row. It is recommend that he have at least seven dry nights before attempting underwear again.

If these measures don't help your child achieve nighttime dryness, you may wish to consider a bedwetting alarm, though such an alarm should not be considered until your child is older than seven or eight years. The bedwetting alarm works by sensing, via small electronic sensor in the underwear when the first drop of urine touches the sensor. The alarm then sounds, waking your child and letting him know it's time to get to the restroom. This, in theory, teaches your child to respond to a full bladder and take appropriate measures (i.e., go to the bathroom). This method boasts a 70 percent success rate after two to three months of use.

Alert

Parents report mixed reviews of the bedwetting alarm. Many state that the whole house woke to the alarm except the person wearing it. If you decide to use this method, you may want to try it in the summer months in order to avoid unnecessary awakenings of other school age children. There are silent alarms that may be utilized as well that vibrate to wake the child upon sensing wetness. This is ideal if you are concerned about waking the entire household.

For the school age child who wets the bed, the medications Imipramine and DDAVP (desmopressin) can be taken for bedwetting. Both are effective in reducing the number of accidents your child has but will only work as long as your child continues to use them. These medications are generally reserved for use on special occasions such as sleepovers, summer camp, and overnight trips. These medicines must be titrated to the right dose for your child and directions must be followed explicitly. If you have strong concerns about your child's bedwetting and want to try medication, seek the advice of your health care provider. Remember, you must be patient; the cure for bedwetting most frequently is the "tincture of time." If your school age child is having accidents during the day, has signs of a urinary tract infection, has blood in his urine, or is experiencing problems with self-esteem, contact your health care provider.

Handling the Naysayers

Choosing to delay potty training your child until she is three years old is likely to draw some swift criticism from your family, particularly your grandparents and possibly your parents. The idea that you will allow your child to wear a diaper long after she is able to talk is a foreign concept to many from previous generations. They may worry about how bad it will look for a four-year-old to be in diapers or how embarrassing it is to have a three-year-old with a smelly diaper. Remember, most people really do mean well when they offer their stories of successful potty training. Unfortunately, often these come across as horrible insults to your parenting style.

Essential

Just as many women want to share their worst pregnancy experiences with pregnant women, many others will want to share their potty-training successes with parents who are preparing to potty train. Do not be discouraged. Remember that phrase, "You are her parent. No one knows her like you do." Your toddler will, at some point, be potty trained.

It is a good idea for you to determine what you would like to use as your reply to those naysayers who will surely have some "words of wisdom" for you at family gatherings. Having a prepared response may alleviate stress and eliminate potential rifts in the fabric of your family. You may try humor in your response, "Yep, the terrible twos really *do* stink!" Or, "My nurse practitioner is pretty sure she won't go to college in diapers." Using an honest, factual approach is always a good option. Be sure that you are convinced of the reasoning behind your decision because, if you waver, this discussion may become stressful. Let this person know that you have researched the ideas of many experts and feel that this method best suits you and your family. (By the way, you may choose a different method with different children in your family. Remember, you are fitting the method to the child's personality.) You may have chosen this method to decrease the amount of stress for your child following a divorce. If so, be sure to inform your critic that the child-oriented approach allows her to have some control in her life since she has already experienced such turmoil. The final "trump" move is that studies have been unable to demonstrate a real correlation between the ages that potty training starts and a successful outcome. And, since you are aware that most children have little physiologic control until age three, there is really no need to rush them into compliance.

Summary of Steps for the Child-Oriented Method

- Evaluate your child's readiness.
- Evaluate your readiness.
- Gather your equipment: potty chair and treats for reinforcements (optional).
- Introduce the potty chair. Make your child comfortable and help him associate the potty chair with the toilet.
- Ask your child to sit on the potty chair fully clothed.
  - Encourage him to sit on the potty chair when you are using the toilet. Explain what you are doing.
  - The potty chair can be used in any room (even outside).
  - Talk or read a story to him while he sits on the potty chair.

- Sit without diaper on potty chair (after one to two weeks spent at step 1) Have him sit only. He does not need to use the potty chair.
  - Empty the stool into the potty chair when he soils his diaper. Explain the reason to him.
  - Begin to take him to the potty chair two to three times per day.
- Practice using the potty chair
  - Remove his diaper for short periods of time. Keep the potty chair handy throughout the day.
  - Encourage him to use the potty chair on his own.
  - Gently remind him throughout the day to use the potty.
- Training pants
  - Teach him to lower and raise training pants or dis posable briefs.

The Pros and Cons of the Slow-Track Method

Pros for the Slower Approach
- Simple concept
- Excellent resources
- Great for parents who employ a more permissive or authoritative style of parenting
- Great for parents and children who have flexible schedules
- Easy for alternate caregivers to follow the plan

Cons for the Slower Approach

- Slow process
- Difficult for parents who prefer a more authoritarian style of parenting
- Requires extended time commitment
- Extends the amount of time your child is in diapers or disposable briefs
- Requires creativity to motivate children to succeed

CHAPTER 6

Motivating Your Child

Chances are good that you are already motivated to potty train your child. You've devoted months and most likely years now to changing diapers, hefting a diaper bag, and basically keeping yourself elbow-deep in your child's digestive system. The time has come for potty training, and you could not be more ready! For your child, however, potty training is a new and scary habit, one with the potential for scolding, embarrassment, and a myriad of other emotional reactions. For that reason, motivation from you, the parent, can only help your child feel more prepared and more excited about her new adventure!

Becoming a Big Kid

The desire to be older starts and ends at an early age, so chances are good your child is already there. She has seen the toys she wants to play with, the playground equipment she wants to climb, and the treatment she wants to receive. She may already be buckling her own car seat, sleeping in a toddler bed, and walking in a store rather than riding in a cart or stroller. These behaviors are good indicators that your child is ready to be a "big kid" and start potty training.

e✔ Fact

If you are thinking about motivating your child, it is important to consider all aspects of the stimulus you use. Many parents recommend candy, others recommend toys, and still others recommend affection and verbal rewards as a means of motivating your child. Your best bet is to experiment with different methods in order to find the most effect motivators for your child.

This is not unlike the methods you use for behaviors you want to encourage. You are likely already using phrases such as, "You have to be a big girl and not cry in the store," "Big girls don't take toys from other kids," and "Big girls know how to keep their hands to themselves and use indoor voices." You may also find yourself using similar phrases in other ways. Phrases like "Only big girls get to play with puppies," "Only big girls can have ice cream after dinner," or even, "Only big girls get to play in the snow," are probably common in your house. These are just a few examples of the many ways in which parents can use the idea of growing up as a way to motivate their child to behave a certain way or respond to a certain incentive. The same is true for potty training!

Essential

Many parents balk at this step. Mothers and fathers alike feel an attachment toward their babies and may reject the idea of encouraging them to adopt a habit that is identified as something for older children. However, potty training is an important step from infancy to early childhood. It is a sign of growing up, so it's important that parents are ready to grow as their children grow up. After all, potty training is only the beginning!

As you use the big kid motivator, make sure you identify each part of potty training as something a big kid would do. The toilet becomes the "Big Kid Potty," and diapers are for babies. Wiping herself becomes a "Big Kid Privilege," unlike babies who have to be cleaned by their parents. Washing her hands with soap and water is just like what a "Big Kid" does after she goes to the bathroom. This constant reminder of the difference between a "big kid" and a baby will not only motivate your child on the most basic level of desires, but it will also help her see potty training as a rite of passage, one where each step is made toward a higher goal.

Becoming Just Like Your Older Sibling/Cousin/Friend

One easy way to alter the big kid method to fit your child is to remind him of his sister, cousin, friend, or another older child he admires. If your child has an older sibling, you have an easy to access, ready-made example. If not, look for other kids who may inspire your child. Just as older kids look up to athletes, actors, and other adults as idols and models of behavior they want to adopt, young toddlers often look to older toddlers and young children to model their own lives after. If you don't have another child in your family, now may be a great time to look at enrolling your child in a preschool program, a playgroup, or even a dance class for toddlers. This will have the added benefit of helping your child with his social skills, sharing, and maybe even learning something new like dance, Tae Kwon Do, or tumbling! By putting him in a situation where he will be around more children, your child will soon start to see his peers using the potty and will want to follow suit. You can and should encourage this behavior. Imagine you are in the store: your child begins throwing a tantrum, and you immediately begin to reprimand him. To do this, you threaten with a time-out, and then you remind him of his friend who got a time-out for having a tantrum in his playgroup. The same method can work for potty training. Finally, using a Big Kid role model will also aid in future motivational steps such as reminding your child about Big Kid underwear, using a Big Kid toilet, and, of course, avoiding the Little Kid changing table.

Choosing Your Own Underwear

One of the most exciting parts of potty training for a child can be the change from the now-cumbersome diaper of babyhood into the new, exciting world of underpants! Although diapers are what your child has always known, the newfound feeling of underwear serves as a physical reminder that she is officially out of diapers and moving into a new stage of maturity and responsibility. Clothing manufacturers have also made underwear more exciting, with a wide variety of styles and graphics available. Boys and girls can be excited by the possibility of wearing the same style of underwear as Mommy or Daddy, but they may also be excited at the chance to pick a style of their very own. Up until this time, you have more than likely chosen most of your child's clothes. Even the pickiest of young girls or the fussiest of young boys frequently has to defer to their parents about what to wear based on weather, events, and various other aspects of the environment. For choosing underwear, however, your child has a chance to take on a very "mature" decision that accompanies her very "mature" role in life as a potty-trained individual. You, as her parent, can now use this opportunity to your advantage.

As you get started on potty training, take your child to the store with you. Show her the wide variety of big girl pants available, and let her choose the style and picture that works best for her. Consider using the toy idols like Barbie or Dora the Explorer to help excite her about the garments. Once she has chosen the pair she likes best, explain to her that she will be allowed to wear her big girl pants every day . . . as soon as she has accomplished potty training, that is. The goal here is not to trick your child, of course, but to show her how responsibilities come with rewards and vice versa. In this scenario, underwear (better known as big girl pants) is very much a reward. The trip to the store, the images, and the choices involved will make buying new big girl pants not unlike buying a new toy!

SARAH, mother to Ben, Patty, and Karen
"Fortunately, all of my children were very conversational at early ages, and I was able to talk to them about the concept of potty training. We went to the store and picked out fabulous underwear for each of them. My son chose He-Man. We talked about how the He-Man underwear was just like Daddy's (only cooler). After many discussions, it took him exactly twenty-four hours and he was potty trained. We didn't spend the entire day focused or anything like that, we had just spent that much time talking about potty training before we switched him to underwear and he just seemed to "get" it. We spent extra time talking about what a shame it would be if he went potty or poopy in his very special underwear, and that really seemed to help."

Working Toward a Larger Goal

A big part of raising an infant, toddler, and child is about teaching your child the art of a process, that steps toward a goal are positive things we should all work on. Potty training is just like reading, math, and other core subjects; it is a process that has an end result. While you and your child both anticipate the end result of a potty-trained child, you should consider offering your child a reward as part of a larger goal. Many parents stop here and state outright that they refuse to bribe their child. Don't think of this as bribery! A larger reward for potty training is similar to an allowance for chores, money for good grades, or a later bedtime in exchange for good behavior.

🅔❗ Alert

It is very important that you only make a promise that you are willing and able to keep. Although this may seem trivial now, and your child may seem young to understand disappointment or distrust, children remember rewards, promises, and regrets at a very young age. Even if he doesn't remember specifically what his part of the promise was, your son is very likely to remember it if he doesn't receive the toy he anticipated and may consider this the next time you offer a reward.

Whatever larger goal reward you choose, you should make sure it fits your family. This can be as small as a Beanie Baby or as large as a tricycle, but it should be a toy that will motivate your child and will appear regularly at a store. Once you and your child have agreed on a toy that will serve as the larger goal, remind him of this reward each time you go to the store (for this reason, it's best to choose a toy that appears at a store you regularly visit with your child). Repeat to him your promise of this toy in exchange for successful potty training. As you do this, make sure to explain your promise to him in terms he will understand. Here is an example of steps to take in a manner he is likely to understand:

1. **Step 1:** Introduce the potty-training process. Whether you have chosen a slow and steady method or baby boot camp, make sure your child understands what you mean by potty training before you begin talking about his eventual reward.

2. **Step 2:** Select the toy. Take your child with you to the store, and allow him to take his time considering the toy or toys he wants the most. Make sure you take responsibility for dissuading him from any toys you are unwilling or unable to buy.

3. **Step 3:** Explain to your child the premises of your promise. Make sure your clearly explain what will qualify as fully potty trained by your standards. This may be a day without a wet or dirty diaper, or you may want an entire week of diaper-free life. The goal is up to you as the parent, but you will be well-served to set a goal that is reasonable and easily understandable for your son.

4. **Step 4:** Take your child to the store with you every time you go. In addition to making good sense in terms of teaching your child how to behave in public, regular visits to the store will serve well as an opportunity for you to remind your child about your promise to him and the agreed-upon reward.

You will want to keep these visits within reason, and your reminders should be uplifting rather than reprimanding. Encourage your child to see his progress toward the toy, and give him an idea of when you anticipate he will be ready for the grand prize. As soon as you have done this, offer to take him to the bathroom! This is a hands-on opportunity to make sure he associates the reward with the responsibility.

5. **Step 5:** Reward time! Because your child is already associating the process with the prize at this point, you will want to make sure you are ready to give him the reward as soon as he has earned it. You may want to have the toy waiting at home in a hidden place, particularly if your child is the impatient type, or you may want to take your child with you to the store in order to buy the toy. By taking your child with you to make the purchase, you are completing the motivational steps that began with taking him to the store, reminding him of the toy, and now giving him the reward he has rightfully earned!

Help Your Child See Progress

Whether or not you choose to use a toy as a long-term reward for a long-term goal, your child will still be interested in seeing her progress over a long period of time. Remember that everything is a learning process for toddlers, including which details to remember, when, and why. This makes potty training another opportunity for you as a parent to help your child look at each day as a stepping stone toward a final goal. Visual rhetoric is best for methods like this, so consider an aid like a star chart.

e✱ Essential

You may find it is better to choose a small goal and a larger goal. For example, perhaps your daughter wants a Barbie and a Barbie Dreamhouse. You could offer her the doll as the reward for one day without a wet or dirty diaper, and then the house could be her reward for an entire week of clean diapers. This will help your daughter understand that, although potty training is important, she will learn it by taking steps toward a bigger goal.

A star chart can actually be any chart you prefer, but something aesthetically pleasing that is typically associated with good behavior often works best when teaching a child. After all, she is already busy learning the entirely new process of potty training, so making her progress chart simple and easy will also make it more effective as a motivating factor. Star charts are frequently used in schools for ages two and up, but it may be best to have your child involved in every step of designing and creating her first star chart. By creating the chart together, your daughter will also gain a hands-on explanation of how a star chart works and the significance of each day and each sticker. You may also want different stickers or stamps for different accomplishments. You may have one sticker for peeing in the potty, another sticker for pooping in the potty, and a third sticker for an entire day of clean diapers. As you begin using your star chart, you may find it works best to allow your child to place her own stickers on as a means of embracing her own reward. This makes getting a sticker each day a cause for celebration.

Diaper-Free Time

Many children love spending time without their clothes on after taking a bath or shower, between clothes and paja-mas, or anytime after they have learned how to remove their own clothing. This clothing-free activity can be used to your advantage! If you are comfortable with it and the weather is compatible, you can use naked time as a reward for your child. However, as with any time when clothing and potty training are involved, there are several factors to consider:

Naked Time as a Reward

Pros	Cons
Enjoyment for your child	May encourage your child to take his clothes off at inappropriate times
Motivation to use the potty	Reliant on temperatures to accommodate a naked child
Less clothing interference when he is ready to use the potty	May involve an accident on your furniture or the floor
Less clothing to be washed if he has an accident	Can only use this method of motivation at home

In order to avoid accidents and still use naked time as a motivating factor, make sure to have your child use the potty before you remove his clothes. Once he has cleared his bladder in the potty, remove his remaining clothes. Some children prefer to only remove their bottoms while others prefer to be completely naked, so, as always, it is best to learn your child's preferences and act accordingly.

⊛ Essential

> It is very important to only begin naked time after your child has used the potty. If you allow naked time after he has soiled his diaper or while you are anticipating his need to use the bathroom, the reward has preceded the responsibility. This breaks the line of association between naked time and using the potty, and he may begin to think he can seek naked time as a reward after peeing or pooping regardless of where he is or whether or not a diaper was involved.

As your child gets older you will likely want to move away from naked time as a reward for using the potty, but children will likely overcome this motivation just as they will outgrow toys and grow tired of activities.

Avoiding Pressure

While rewards can be a fun and easy way to motivate your child toward potty training, it is important to remember that rewards should be a pleasant prize for a job well done.

While this may seem like obvious information, parents often run the risk of using rewards as a means for pressuring their children into acquiring a behavior or habit they are either not yet old enough to handle or simply need more time to develop. By now you have learned that, regardless of the number of potty-training methods you use with your child, she will not be diaper-free until she is ready. Rewards do not change this. Your child may be old enough to play with the toys of her choice, wear the underwear of her choice, or remove her clothes when she wants, but that does not necessarily mean she is old enough for potty training.

With this fact in mind, it is your responsibility to avoid pressuring your child into potty training before she is ready. The promise of a reward for a behavior she cannot yet achieve will only serve as a punishment for something she cannot control if you try to begin potty training before she is ready. The result can be further anguish for her when she has an accident, excessive frustration with her own body, and even immunity toward future rewards.

Just as it is important for you to avoid pressuring your child into a behavior she cannot yet handle, it is also important to make sure you are not putting too much pressure on yourself. Potty training is a team effort, which means that if a child is taking longer to potty train or is not ready to do so at an expected age, it is not always the fault of the parent. Similarly, parents often feel they need to push potty training in order to put their child in a certain preschool, day care, or group activity program. While these institutions have an understandable right to require children to be potty trained before accepting them into the program, this does not mean that all children should be potty trained at a certain time. For example, let's say you want to enroll your three year-old in swimming lessons, but she has not yet mastered potty training. The gym that runs the lessons insists that all children be potty trained before they participate, so your daughter won't be ready when the lesson starts like the other ten children in the class. This does not mean your child is behind or that the other parents have done something you have not. After all, for these ten toddlers who are potty trained, there are thousands more who, like your daughter, are not yet ready for lessons that require being potty trained. Take a deep breath and relax. Remember, despite multiple threats from parents and numerous family jokes, hardly any children actually attend their high school graduation in diapers.

Fact

If your child approaches her fourth birthday and is still struggling with potty training, you may want to consult your pediatrician about possible contributing factors. Issues such as attention-deficit disorder, attention-deficit/hyperactivity disorder, and others that can contribute to your child's delayed potty-training. While there are many possibilities, it is important to speak to your pediatrician before attributing potty-training complications to any specific learning delay.

As you avoid putting unnecessary pressure on yourself, it is also important to be willing to try different methods for different children without expecting the same result every time.

PATTY JO, mother to Sarah, Shannon, and Scott
"We started potty training when our daughter was newly one year old. We used rewards, praise, reading books, a potty chair in whatever room we were in, more praise, big girl pretty panties, popsicle rewards, and more praise while she was learning to pull the panties down, wiping, and pulling them up. It took one month. Our second child, a daughter, had the same success. (And just so you don't go away thinking I'm a genius, this did not work with our third child, a son. He was three years old before he decided for himself that he didn't want to start preschool in diapers.) Two out of three isn't bad."

The Reality of Rewards

As wonderful as rewards sound as the miracle ingredient in potty training, they are not without their risks. Just as you expect a paycheck for every day you work because that is the compromise you agreed upon and the reward you have come to expect, toddlers also begin to associate behaviors with rewards on a continual pattern until they "expect" a reward. This often leads to a sense of entitlement for current and future behaviors.

Some possible complications from rewards include:

- Unreasonable expectations
- Attachment to unhealthy rewards
- Unavailable rewards
- Entitlement

Unreasonable Expectations

The problem: As your child grows accustomed to receiving rewards, he may also grow bored with one reward, which will prompt you to seek an alternative reward. You may start with a sticker, for example, but then find yourself moving on to a small toy or a trip to the playground. Soon your child grows tired of these rewards, so you turn to food, larger toys, or longer trips to the playground. Before you know it, your child's rewards have become beyond reasonable expectation or ability. You may find yourself unable to keep him pleased with the rewards you do have available, and you may find yourself unable to acquire a better reward.

The solution: Variety is the spice of life. Before the rewards become a problem, start pursuing a solution. Consider having a variety of rewards available, and make it a game to determine which reward he gets at any given bathroom time. You might keep small snacks, toys, and stickers in a bag that he gets to draw from after using the bathroom. You might also create a spinning wheel that he can spin to determine which reward he gets. Another possibility is to have him close his eyes and hold out his hands while you choose the treat for him. Whichever method you choose, a reward can often maintain its value as a reward if it is also a surprise. He knows the act he must perform in order to receive his reward, but the reward he gets is anybody's guess!

Unhealthy Attachments

Problem: Many parents choose to use something sweet like chocolate, cookies, or other types of candy in order to motivate their children. While it is a good idea to use a reward that your children genuinely want, it is also important to consider the long-term effects. Childhood obesity is on the rise and can lead to early onset diabetes, high cholesterol, high blood pressure, and more. Childhood is also a time when children learn behaviors they will carry with them into adulthood, so now is an important time to refrain from teaching your children to associate basic responsibilities with sugary rewards. This does not mean that chocolate can *never* be used as a reward or that your children should *never* be allowed to eat sugar. Moderation is key, whether it be in your own diet or your child's. As you are preparing a variety of treats to be available for rewards, make sure that sugar is only one of many options. You should also make sure your sugary treats are only available at appropriate times. For example, if your three year-old shows a partiality for pixie sticks, you probably do not want them to get candy as a reward right before bedtime.

Solution: The decision regarding when and how much sugar your child receives as a reward is ultimately up to you, but remember that children are often equally pleased with a sweet apple, naturally sugary juice, or even just a small part of a larger piece of candy as a reward. You may also decide that food is simply not the best means to reward your child. There are many other rewards—including special activities, a trip to the store, time at the playground, and stickers—that can take the place of sugary treats.

Unavailable Rewards

Problem: Because parenting is a full-time job, potty training is also a full-time job. As you find yourself closer to a diaper-free life, your child will begin communicating with you more often about when he needs to go to the bathroom, regardless of where you are. You have to help your child understand that bathrooms are everywhere. You will find yourself using more public restrooms even as you help your child learn how to "hold it." However, your child may not always understand that rewards are not always available, or he may decide that it is not worth his time, attention, and effort to use a toilet in a place where there is no reward.

Solutions: The first solution is to include extra rewards in the bag of supplies you have to carry otherwise. As you know by now, even after you have freed yourself from the cumbersome diaper bag, you still have to keep supplies for a change of clothes, possible snacks, and more. Including a few small rewards in this bag will help you and your child maintain a consistent motivation method for potty training. If you choose to keep rewards with you, make sure you consider which rewards will best fit in with your daily routine.

Another possible solution is to teach your child that rewards are not always available. You can either teach him that he will receive a reward when he gets home, a method that will encourage patience and understanding, or you may simply teach him that he will not get a reward every time he uses a toilet. While this is a viable solution, consistent rules are typically easier for children to understand than varying rules. This means that, while you may find it awkward or burdensome to carry rewards with you in addition to all of your other parenting supplies, it may be more effective than the alternative solutions.

Entitlement

Problem: Many parents who have used rewards to help motivate their child for potty training have found later that their children begin to expect rewards for all positive behaviors. As you teach your child about potty training as a Big Kid responsibility, he will likely remember the language you have used as well as the basic idea that responsibilities equal rewards. As you incorporate more responsibilities—such as picking up his toys, behaving well in stores, and minding his manners with adults—he may begin asking for, or even demanding, his reward for everyday, run-of-the-mill Big Kid responsibilities.

Solution: What you already know and your child needs to learn is that rewards come in all forms. A reward for potty training likely comes in the form of a more explicit reward such as a new toy for many reasons. After all, your child is younger, the responsibility is more difficult, and the goal is rewarding for you and him. With other behaviors, however, you have more lessons to teach your child. The first lesson is the built-in reward. If he picks up his toys, he gets to play with more toys. If he behaves well in the store, he gets to keep going to the store. And the list goes on. The point is that he has already been enjoying the privileges that come with what are now his responsibilities. Therein lies the second lesson: some responsibilities are just part of being a big kid. Big kids behave themselves in public places because that is their responsibility, and your son will need to follow suit. He may resist these responsibilities at first, but over time he will learn that you cannot reward him every time he does something he is supposed to do. You can also help him by showing him your own responsibilities that may or may not come with rewards.

CHAPTER 7

Nighttime Dryness: Handling Bedwetting

If you have made it this far, it's likely that your child has already had several days of waking up dry from her naps. Likely she has even woken dry in the morning at least once in the past few days. If your child has bladder control during the day, she probably will have bladder control at night also. It is important for you to know, however, that she may be experiencing some beginner's luck. Just as there are bumps in the road with all other developmental milestones most children will have accidents during the potty-training process. And of course, some will have more accidents than others.

Encouraging Nighttime Dryness

After your child has achieved daytime dryness, it is time to begin encouraging nighttime dryness. This nighttime dryness depends on the size of your child's bladder as well as his muscle strength. If you have potty trained a two-year-old boy and he is experiencing daytime dryness, he may continue to have some nighttime accidents. Do not be discouraged by this; it is very important to remember that no child wets the bed on purpose. It is truly an accident. Your child may be a sound sleeper, and therefore he sleeps through cues for bladder emptying. His bladder may be growing slowly and is therefore unable to accommodate urine produced overnight. Other reasons for nighttime elimination, ones that occur less frequently, are physical abnormalities or hormone deficiencies that prevent nighttime dryness.

It is important to maximize your sleepy child's ability to get to a potty at night by eliminating any obstacles to dryness. So, if you are not ready to go "cold turkey" from something absorbent, use a disposable brief instead of a diaper. These garments allow for easy removal, especially in the case of a sleepy toddler. If your child is younger than age three, it is unlikely that he is fearful of the dark. However, he may be reluctant to walk through a darkened hallway at night and so you may wish to move the potty chair into his room. If this idea isn't appealing to you, use multiple nightlights to light the path from his bed to the bathroom.

It is really important to consider your child's sleeping arrangement as you move forward. Children in toddler beds should be able to get out of bed without problems. However, if the toddler bed has a side rail to prevent rolling out of the bed in the middle of the night, your child may struggle with getting to the potty in time. Many parents are opting to transition their child from the crib to a full size bed, and this can present some challenges. For example, those short little legs struggle to find the floor in the middle of the night. You may consider having your child sleep on a mat next to his bed until he is able to establish his nighttime habits.

Accidents

Most children begin to stay dry overnight sometime around three years of age, which, incidentally, coincides with the time most children recognize the need to urinate and have bowel movements. Bedwetting (nocturnal enuresis) is one of the most common symptoms experienced by children between ages three and thirteen years. It is estimated that as many as five to seven million children in the United States continue to wet the bed beyond the age of six. In fact, bedwetting often runs in families. Approximately 77 percent of all children who have nighttime accidents have two first degree relatives who also had problems with bedwetting. Therefore, if Mom and Dad were bedwetters, the child has a greater chance of becoming a bedwetter. If you or your spouse had nighttime accidents, your odds of having a child who experiences the same goes up by 43 percent. In children with no family history of bedwetting, 15 percent will have nighttime accidents. In order to truly reach the diagnosis of bedwetting, your child must be wetting at night at least twice per week for three months in a row. It is this persistence that causes many parents to become concerned about their children.

Nighttime accidents affect boys more often and for a longer time than girls. It has been proposed that, since continence is linked to developmental maturity, girls may experience fewer problems since they tend to mature faster, on average, than boys.

How Should You Handle Accidents?

Bedwetting can be a hugely frustrating problem for parents. You are faced with not only cleaning your little darling up after the accident, but also washing an extra load of laundry just as you were rushing out of the house to work.

You are most certainly taking your child to the potty before naptime already, and this is often the only needed solution to accidents at naptime. Nighttime can be an entirely different issue. One proposed solution is to wake the child at night and carry her to the potty. The Brazelton method describes this as additional pressure on the child, and this has the potential to backfire as children may respond by holding urine in an attempt to control the situation. And guess what happens next? Another accident!

A second suggestion for preventing nighttime accidents is to limit fluid intake before bed. In order to have an effect, your child should have her last drink approximately two hours before bedtime. This is extremely difficult when you are not able to eat dinner until 6:00 PM or later and your child goes to bed by 7:00 PM. By age five, children can typically consume as many as eight ounces of fluid prior to bedtime without difficulty. However, in younger children this may be too much for their smaller bladders to accommodate. It is important to remember that limiting fluids during the day can be very harmful for your child; she may become constipated creating even more problems for going to the potty.

Fact

Training Tip: Keep a night light on in the hallway and bathroom to ensure your child's safety as she navigates waking and walking at night.

Another suggestion is to have your child go to the bathroom just as her bedtime routine begins and return to the bathroom just before she gets into bed. This is a good option but has mixed results. Some feel that urinating frequently during the day does not allow for adequate expansion of the bladder, thereby reducing its capacity overnight.

One other option is to have a reward system for dry nights similar to the one you may have used to achieve daytime dryness. Children tend to be motivated by those tangible rewards. You may wish to set goals for successes along the way with a bigger goal for accomplishing consistent night time dryness.

 Fact

> Key Point: Keep in mind that as many as 10 percent of all five-year-olds continue to have nighttime accidents and as much as 5 percent of all ten-year-olds have nighttime accidents.

Lastly, you may ask a child who is three or older to participate in cleaning up her own accident. This helps her realize her responsibility for an action. Remember, this should not be a punishment to her. You are in the teaching and training role, helping her develop a sense of autonomy as she is able to place the soiled sheets in the washer. Try to allow your child to participate in as many steps as she can physically handle, but don't let her handle any detergents or cleansers. Once the laundry has finished washing, allow your child to transfer the clothes to the dryer, place the dryer sheet in the drum, close the door, and press the start button. Once the sheets and clothes are clean and dry, allow her to help replace the clean sheets on the bed. As your child helps you with the laundry, you will be able to teach more than just responsibility. You can review colors, shapes, and sorting. This is a great way to build her ability to match and problem solve.

It is possible that your child will have a subsequent accident just to have the chance to do laundry again. There are worse things that can happen, and those laundry skills will benefit you and your household for years to come. You may, however, need to discuss this and find other ways for your child to help with laundry.

It is difficult not to become angry when your child repeatedly wets the bed. However, it is very important that you do not. Wet sheets are one thing; your child's self esteem is another. Children who are scolded or punished following accidents are at risk for serious long-term emotional problems. Conversely, children who are long-term bedwetters but have supportive parents and are free from shame and doubt emerge with no psychological impact. Children will, as they get older, realize that their siblings and friends are not wetting the bed at night. Suddenly your preschooler is ashamed about having accidents. It is important that you remain positive in this instance and make sure your child knows that you understand she is neither wetting on purpose nor is she just lazy. In addition, make sure that your extended family does not tease her about bed wetting. In fact, there is really no need to discuss nighttime accidents in front of anyone else. This helps your child know that you are trustworthy.

There are really two schools of thought related to overnight and naptime accidents. On the one hand, you are trying to help your child recognize the need to get to a potty as soon as she feels the first sign of wetness. Diapers or disposable briefs may be so absorbent that she cannot recognize wetness on her skin. On the other hand, accidents are bound to happen. Do you really want to wash bed linens several times each day? A Pull-Up or diaper may save you several loads of laundry and frustration.

Most of the parenting books you will find in press today will discourage you from returning to diapers after having been in panties or underwear. This is, in part, due to concerns over whether or not your child's self esteem is damaged by the return to diapers. There is really no reason to continue to be frustrated with your child and have persistent interrupted sleep due to those middle-of-the-night sheet changes. She is just as miserable as you are when she must wake from sleep, wash herself or be washed with a cold cloth or wipe, and change into dry clothes.

Why Does Bedwetting Occur?

Nocturnal enuresis is divided into two categories: primary enuresis and secondary enuresis. Primary enuresis typically describes the child who has some dry nights but cannot go for a full month without having an accident. It is unclear why these children do not wake to go to the potty, but it is often related to fatigue, family stress, divorce, or a new baby. Children who are dry every night for a month and then have an accident are likely to be classified as having secondary enuresis.

Bedwetting is not a behavior problem in most cases, nor does it happen because of laziness. However, in addition to some of the reasons previously discussed in this chapter, bedwetting may occur for a variety of other reasons. One reason is related to stress; the arrival of a new baby, a divorce, or a family upset may cause an increase in accidents (day and night). You may expect an older child to regress when a baby is born. He is trying to decide if he wants to grow up or be a baby all at the same time. He wants your attention, be it positive or negative, and he will do whatever it takes to get it. So, if you feel that he is capable of getting to the potty but wants you to notice him, show him positive attention in other ways. Perhaps you could schedule one-on-one time away from the new baby. Give him special jobs around the house and over overwhelming praise for a job well done. You want to emphasize the difference between positive behavior and negative behavior in terms of the attention he will get from you.

 Alert

Prolonged bedwetting can be caused by a nerve disease like spina bifida. Spina bifida is a birth defect in which the vertebrae fail to enclose the entire spinal column. It's not a condition that is always obvious, since there are usually no problems with the child's range of motion, muscle tone, and general appearance. It is often discovered around the time toilet training begins when parents notice that their children cannot maintain dryness in between trips to the potty, and certainly not overnight. If you have concerns about your child's frequent wetness, contact your pediatrician.

If the increase in accidents is related to a recent move or a parental divorce, your child is likely feeling insecure or fearful. It is important to reassure children that they are safe and loved. In the case of divorce, one of the most important things you can do to reassure your child is to refrain from negative discussions of your (ex) spouse while the child is present. Help him understand that the divorce was not his fault and that both parents love him very much. If you have recently moved and are experiencing an increase in accidents, allow your child to be an active member of the "moving team." By accomplishing chores associated with the move (e.g., stacking toilet paper under the bathroom counter, placing underwear in drawers, etc.) your child will develop a more secure feeling of his new surroundings. If, however, there are areas that are unfamiliar, he may continue to harbor feelings of insecurity.

As stated previously, most children no longer experience nighttime accidents after the age of six. Thus, prior to this age there is little advantage to treating a child for bedwetting. If your child is still wetting the bed beyond age four, be assured it is likely related to other causes and not typically a kidney or bladder problem. In addition to social stressors, bedwetting may be related to a sleep disorder as studies show a correlation between snoring or disordered breathing and nocturnal enuresis. If you are concerned about your child's snoring, speak with your pediatric health care provider. You may then be referred to a specialist for further evaluation.

Increasing accidents or a return of accidents following an extended period of dryness may be due to the presence of infection. If you notice a foul odor to your child's urine, there may be a urinary tract infection (UTI) that warrants a trip to the clinic. Left untreated, lower tract infections can progress into the upper urinary tract (kidneys) causing irreversible damage. Your primary pediatric care provider will have your child urinate in a sterile container and perform a urinalysis and culture to evaluate whether or not there are bacteria in the urine. Then, depending on the results, she may prescribe antibiotic for your child.

Question

When should you have your child's bedwetting be evaluated by a pediatric health care provider?
Your child's inability to stay dry should be evaluated if he is over six years old and is still bedwetting every night, if he is bothered by his bedwetting (even if he is younger than six years), if he has experienced a sudden return of nighttime accidents, if you are frustrated and overwhelmed by his bedwetting, if you have punished your child or are worried that you might punish your child for wetting the bed, or if your child has had a sudden recurrence of daytime accidents.

Managing Prolonged Bedwetting

The longer your child has nighttime accidents, the higher her risk for being found out at school. This kind of "outing" may result in her being excluded from attending activities with friends. Additionally, the longer a parent has to deal with wet sheets, soiled clothing, and carpet stains, the more intolerant of accidents that parent becomes. At this time there are no studies that show bedwetting leads directly to low self-esteem, but there are studies that demonstrate that children who are bedwetters appear to feel bad about themselves. Thus, helping your child achieve nighttime dryness is always the goal. Almost all of the treatment and management strategies currently in use are designed to help your child recognize when her bladder is full or to decrease the need for her to void at night.

 **Essential**

> Key point: Overcoming bedwetting is not a priority goal until after the age of six years. Remember, most children will outgrow nocturnal enuresis by this age without any intervention.

If your child is over six years old and continues to wet the bed, it is important to have a full medical exam by your pediatric primary care provider. She will be able to rule out any physical condition that could be contributing to the accidents such as infection, constipation, and any nerve disease. She may also be able to determine if genetics or family stressors have had an impact on the continued or resumed bedwetting. It remains critical for you to continue responding to your child with patience and compassion when it comes to bedwetting. In fact, the less emphasis you place on nighttime accidents, the less stress, shame, and guilt felt by your child.

As discussed previously in this chapter, one of the least stressful ways in which to attempt to control nighttime accidents is to limit fluids. Although this is the most recommended "cure" to bedwetting, it is somewhat controversial among providers and parents alike. There is little evidence to show that fluid restriction affects bedwetting at all. Even so, avoiding large amounts of fluid at night or just prior to bedtime *is* a good idea. Drinking a "normal" amount of fluid in the evening has not been shown to impact nocturnal enuresis. It is important to eliminate any caffeinated drinks (soda, tea, etc.) since these are known bladder irritants and can cause more frequent urination.

Bladder Training

Bladder training is an option for training children with nocturnal enuresis. However, this is strategy is fraught with controversy. Bladder capacity in children is reported to increase one ounce (30ml) each year during the first eight years of life. Girls tend to have a larger capacity than boys do. (This may be another factor contributing to why bedwetting is more common in little boys than it is in little girls). Bladder training requires an increased amount of fluid intake during the day and continued encouragement to help your child hold her urine for longer periods of time. First you will have her attempt to hold urine for an extra few minutes before she uses the potty. You gradually increase this time until she is able to hold the urine longer. This will increase bladder capacity and improve muscle strength in the sphincters that determine flow of urine. Increasing the bladder capacity will not only help with nighttime dryness but also daytime dryness.

e✱ Essential

Bedwetting alarms are another option for treating bedwetting. The alarm has a moisture sensor that is placed in your child's underwear. The sensor is attached to a speaker that is attached with Velcro to the shoulder of her pajamas. The alarm is designed to sound at the first drop of moisture in the underwear. See Chapter 5 for more information.

Lifting

Lifting is a strategy used by many parents to manage their children's nocturnal enuresis. Lifting merely means that the parent takes the child to the potty at the same time each night. She will encourage the child to void and then return the child to bed without ever fully waking the child. This strategy is not only time-consuming, but also not very effective because it may encourage continued bed wetting as the child continues to void while "sleeping." It also prevents the child from experiencing a full bladder since parents learn to take the child to the potty before the accident occurs in bed. Some parents choose to modify this strategy and wake their child to go to the potty. This may be a little more effective, but some experts argue that this only causes the child to become reliant on someone or something to wake up. Obviously, if you have already tried this strategy and experienced positive results, there is really no reason for you to change your course.

Guided Imagery

Some parents choose hypnotherapy or guided imagery as ways to help children who sleep deeply achieve nighttime dryness. Many have found hypnosis to be an effective way to treat bedwetting, but you can't administer it on your own; you will need to find a trained therapist. The therapist may provide recordings for your child to listen to on a daily basis. Hypnosis works by having the child listen repeatedly to a hypnosis recording, reprogramming the brain to help the child respond to a full bladder when she is asleep and awake. Guided imagery, however, can be performed by anyone. Here is how you do it:

1. Tell your child to relax, and close her eyes. She must listen to what you say
2. Explain to your child that her kidneys are designed to make urine all day and night
3. Let her know that her bladder is a holding place for urine and it is safe there until she is ready to go to the potty
4. Explain that there is a muscle that is very important. It holds her urine in the bladder until she is ready to potty
5. Help her understand that she controls the muscle very well during the day but seems to be having

some problems with controlling the muscle at night. Some of the urine is sneaking out

6. During the night, she is going to start being more in control of her urine

7. Help her understand that her new job is to help her bladder when it is full. She will start controlling the muscle when she is asleep, just like she does when she is awake

8. She will potty in the bathroom at night when she is ready

If you continue to give your child messages like these, her brain will respond with an increased awareness of the need to get up and go to the potty. You should discontinue guided imagery if you do not notice an improvement within two weeks.

Medications

Medications are another way to treat nocturnal enuresis, and there are three in particular that may be prescribed for bedwetting. The first medication is Desmopressin or DDAVP an anti-diuretic hormone that suppresses the need for urination overnight. It is used to control but will not cure bedwetting. Older children and those with larger bladder capacity tend to respond more favorably to DDAVP. Desmopressin is available in a nasal spray and tablet form, but the nasal spray was recently placed under a ban by the FDA from use in treating nocturnal enuresis. The tablet form, however, is still used successfully in children. It is not intended for daily use, but is rather a great temporary therapy for use on special occasions such as slumber parties and summer camp. The use of DDAVP does not come without some risk. Side effects may include dry mouth, headache, nausea, and abdominal pain, but none of these are commonly reported. When your child is prescribed DDAVP, fluids must be restricted two hours before bedtime due to the risk of overfilling the bladder.

Another medication that may be used for bedwetting is Imipramine. Imipramine, or Tofranil, is a tricyclic antidepressant that has been used for many years with great success. In fact, between 10–50 percent of those children treated with Imipramine report complete nighttime dryness. It is commonly prescribed for bedwetting and has been shown to be helpful in older children. It is not well understood why Imipramine works so well for bedwetting. It is believed to work in one of three ways: 1) by altering your child's sleep wake pattern; 2) by affecting the length of time your child can hold her urine; or 3) by reducing the amount of urine produced overnight. Usually the child takes the dose one to two hours prior to bedtime. Most children taking Imipramine don't experience side effects. However, there are several side effects of using this medication including mood changes, nightmares, dry mouth, confusion, dizziness, drowsiness, cardiac arrhythmias, and others.

A third medication that is used for children who wet the bed is oxybutynin or Ditropan. Oxybutynin is an anticholinergic medication that works by decreasing bladder contractions and increasing bladder capacity. This medication is especially useful in children who have daytime accidents. Using an anticholinergic has not proven successful in children who have nighttime wetness only.

This Too Shall Pass

While you are going through the trials and tribulations of helping your child achieve nighttime dryness, keep a positive attitude. Your child watches you and your response to his accidents will undoubtedly have an effect on him. Remember, he already feels shame and guilt when he does not have a dry night, so he doesn't need you to remind him of his accident. It is especially important that your child not be punished in any way following a wet night. The long-term effects of punishing your child may be seen as low self-esteem in later years. It may be difficult for you to hide your frustration while you are washing sheets for the fifth time during the week. Hide it! He did not do this to you or on purpose. No one wants to stay dry more than he does.

As a parent you assume many different roles throughout the life of your child: caregiver, comforter, protector, teacher, mentor, and many others. Perhaps none is more important than "coach" during the potty-training season. This season may be short or long. It may be characterized by several successes and occasional failures. A good coach remains a positive role model and influence at all times. Most certainly the coach feels disappointed when the player does not deliver, but the coach cannot let it show. A good coach believes in the player when the player does not believe in himself even though there are times he may feel let down too! As you continue this journey, remember the role of the parent coach. It will be helpful in many ways, especially in the years after potty training.

Essential

There are many websites that have excellent information on bedwetting, such as those hosted by children's hospitals, government sponsored sites, and physician groups such as the American Academy of Pediatrics (AAP). It is important that you consider the source you are reading before adopting everything it claims.

In summary, keep up the good work. You and your child will soon be past this phase of his life and you will be all the wiser. Thankfully, many of the harder things you experience are ultimately forgotten (e.g. pregnancy, childbirth, potty training). So, just when you are ready to throw in the towel, don't. Your child will suddenly no longer need disposable briefs, bed alarms, or medication. He will be dry on more nights than he is wet until the magical day when he is able to sleep in underwear without the concern of waking wet. You both will have done it!

Points to Remember

- Bedwetting is a normal part of potty training.
- Normal healthy children may wet the bed.

- Bedwetting is often hereditary.
- Prolonged bedwetting can be a sign of infection or other problems.
- Most children are nighttime dry by the time they are five years old.
- Scolding and punishment for accidents is not helpful in ending bedwetting.
- Children over seven years who are still bedwetting may wish to seek consultation from their primary pediatric care provider.
- Bladder training, bedwetting alarms, and medicines may be used to treat bedwetting.
- Most children will outgrow bedwetting naturally.
- Limit (or avoid completely) any drinks with caffeine.
- Take your child to the bathroom just prior to bedtime.
- Use disposable briefs as long as necessary. This is not an admission of defeat!

CHAPTER 8

When Bad Accidents Happen to Good Kids

Okay, by now you've been through a fair portion of the potty training. You've chosen the method that best suits your lifestyle, and you are rejoicing in your soon-to-be diaper-free life. As you make your way out into the world, free of the once burdensome diaper bag, you congratulate yourself on a job well done. Suddenly you feel the telltale warmth spreading not far from the hand where you are supporting your diaper-free child. Accidents are a fact of life and, no matter how many people tell you their children never had accidents because they used a certain method of potty training, the fact of the matter is that you as the parent of a potty-trained child must be prepared for accidents.

Accidents Happen

Besides your own upset over the accident and what this means for the rest of your day (and the rest of your diaper bag-carrying days), it is important for you to focus on what this means for your child. She may be experiencing a myriad of emotions now including anger, embarrassment, or sorrow. On the other hand, she may not even be aware yet that she has had an accident. To say that parents often get frustrated at the first sign of an accident is an understatement, and this is why it is important to make sure you do not convey your frustration to your child. She needs to be as aware as you are that accidents happen and, although this does not mean accidents should happen, they also should not serve as a means for regression, punishment, or humiliation.

As you determine how you are going to handle accidents with your child, you should also consider the age at which you began potty training. If you have a particularly advanced eighteen-month-old who has already begun potty training, you need to remember that potty training at such a young age (or any age, for that matter) is not a sure thing. She may go weeks without having a wet diaper, and then wet her pants just as you change her into underwear. Again, accidents happen. At this age, she may not be ready to understand your verbal communication regarding her accident, and so you may be better off leaving her in diapers for a while longer. By the same token, a four-year-old is preparing to start kindergarten soon and likely has a higher sense of urgency for when she must be finished with potty training. A four-year-old should not be punished any more than an eighteen-month-old for having an accident, but now would be a good time for you to sit down with your child and have a discussion about what it means to have accidents and how you can avoid them in the future.

Accidents as a Learning Experience

As you prepare to address these accidents with your child, consider using them as a learning experience. You as the parent have learned the importance of carrying supplies with you even after you feel your child's potty training is complete. You may not need diapers anymore, but you will still need many other items to help prepare you for the potential, and often inevitable, accident.

Supplies for Before Potty Training
- Diapers (at least three)
- Rash cream
- Wipes
- Two clean onesies/shirts
- Two clean pants/bottoms
- Extra socks
- Changing pad (reusable or disposable)
- Plastic bags (for particularly dirty diapers)

Supplies for After Potty Training
- Underwear (at least one)
- Wipes

- One clean shirt
- One clean pair of pants/bottoms
- Extra socks
- Plastic bags

Many people look at a list like this and immediately begin crossing items off. After all, the fewer the items you carry, the smaller the bag and the smaller the load on your shoulder. Additionally, many people feel they can rely on the supplies of the average public bathroom. It's just one day, right? The truth of the matter is that you are not just preparing for one afternoon or even one day out and about with your child. Instead, you are preparing for the possibility of a pee accident, a poop accident, a diarrhea accident, and more. You have to be ready for a leaky accident that may affect socks and shoes, just as you have to be ready for poop that necessitates more involved cleanup that will require the wipes of the old days.

 **Essential**

> Some parents are especially lucky and never have to use many of the supplies on this list. Hopefully you are one of these parents, but the old adage, "better to be safe than sorry," still applies. The more prepared you are for an accident, the less the accident will affect your overall day.

Now that you see the accident as a learning experience for yourself—and hopefully one to be avoided—

it is important to consider this mishap to be a learning experience for your child as well. Criticizing, punishing, or otherwise reprimanding your child for having an accident will not only not help the situation, but these actions may even result in further regression in the potty-training process. Using a toilet is such a new and unusual activity for toddlers that creating negative attitudes will only work to further distance you from your goal of a diaper-free life.

A good example is when you taught your child not to bite. Most small children, from infants to toddlers, go through a stage where they find biting to be a way to express emotions and convey frustration. Biting is also an activity that can usually be discouraged rather quickly, but it usually involves reprimanding, punishment of some form, and further serious talks from a parent. These actions typically (although not always) work to dissuade a child from biting further, so many parents feel the same actions should work to discourage their children from having accidents. One key difference between potty training and biting, however, is that biting is a chosen, controlled action. Short of falling on top of someone with his mouth open, it is virtually impossible for your child to "accidentally" bite someone. Bedwetting, diaper wetting, and other elimination incidents are referred to as "accidents" because that's exactly what they are: unintentional occurrences. If your child is still potty training, that means he is still learning how and when to control his bladder. He is also learning to *remember* to control his bladder, which means he is going to have accidents sometimes. Because these are not actions your child typically chooses to take, punishments will often lead to confusion, fear, and, ultimately, more accidents.

One Mom's Accident Story

"I spent months potty training my son when he was three and we were finally out of diapers. We tried everything, but it just took forever for him to be potty trained! We offered rewards, tried spending days at home where we did nothing without constantly going to the bathroom. We put potty chairs in multiple rooms in the house, including his bedroom and his playroom. Nothing worked! When he finally stopped wearing diapers, it seemed to us all that he was finally potty trained. He hadn't peed in his diaper in over three weeks, and he hadn't pooped in his diaper in almost two weeks. Hallelujah! To celebrate, I took him to the mall to buy a treat.

"I spoke too soon. While we were in the store, he was beside himself with excitement over a new tricycle, and the next thing I knew there was a yellow puddle surrounding my son. He had peed in the store while we were picking out his toy! I was furious. I yelled at him and told him that he should be embarrassed. We left the store without his toy, and he cried the whole way home. By the time he was clean and changed, I felt awful for what I had done. He was excited, and it was probably my fault for not making sure he had emptied his bladder when I knew he was going to be so excited. I apologized as soon as he got up from his nap, and then I talked to him about how to make sure that doesn't happen in the future. We've had a few accidents since then, but that was the last time I was responsible for making him feel bad about nature calling."

—*Teresa, mother to John, age 4*

How to Handle Accidents

Unfortunately, accidents can be such a source of frustration for parents that it is often hard enough to maintain your patience while reacting to the situation, much less manage to use the accident as a learning experience. Fortunately, there is a pattern you can use when handling accidents that will help you remember to stay calm while also teaching your child about how to avoid accidents in the future.

STEP 1: ASK YOUR CHILD IF HE IS HAVING AN ACCIDENT

By calling this an accident rather than asking him if he is peeing or pooping (as you probably did while he was still in diapers), you are already noting a difference between going to the bathroom in a diaper or in a bathroom versus in underpants. This question also serves to call your child's attention to both what is happening and his involvement in it. Unless he has been asking to go to the bathroom and you have not yet made it to one, chances are good that he has not even realized what is happening!

STEP 2: TAKE HIM TO A BATHROOM.

Although many parents feel that their children should have to endure the wetness of their pants after having accidents, such a method can also lead to humiliation, a desire to return to a diaper (when accidents were not so uncomfortable), and resentment. In addition to saving your child the anguish and discomfort of wet pants, you will also be rescuing the rest of the world from similar discomforts! As important as it is for you to teach your child about when and how to properly prevent accidents, your fellow shoppers, friends, or family more than likely do not want to participate.

Your child's hygiene is an equally—if not more—important reason not to prolong having him sit in wet pants. As you likely experienced in the form of diaper rashes during your child's infant/early toddler years, the uric acid that comes in pee can be damaging to your child's skin. He may still experience diaper rashes (called thus because of the area where the rash occurs, even if it does not come as a result of a diaper), discomfort, raw skin, and more if he spends an extended period of time in wet pants. Changing him quickly and cleaning with your traditional diaper wipes can help reduce the chances of a diaper rash, but if your child has particularly sensitive skin you may still want to treat him with a topical cream to help prevent the possibility of a future rash developing.

STEP 3: ASK YOUR CHILD WHY HE DID NOT ASK TO GO TO A BATHROOM.

By asking him why he did not ask rather than simply reminding him to ask, you are once again attributing the responsibility of potty training to your child. In the early

stages of potty training it is your responsibility to continu-
ally ask your child if he needs to go to the bathroom, and
even take him to the bathroom on some occasions when
he says it is not necessary. As you transition into your
diaper-free life, it is equally important to teach your child
that it is now his responsibility to ask for a bathroom as
well. When you ask your child why he did not ask to go
to the bathroom, you do not want to sound as though you
are reprimanding him. Instead, this should be the first part
in a mature, intelligent conversation you have with him
about what happened and how to prevent it from happening again.

If your child did ask for a bathroom and you were
unable to get him to a toilet in time, you may need to consider how much of the fault rests with your child before
you continue the conversation. Just as children frequently
have accidents because they get distracted or overly
excited and "forget" to go to the bathroom, parents frequently make the same mistakes. Whether you are in a
store that does not have a bathroom, involved in a conversation that cannot go into the restroom with you, or
even hoping you can make it home before he goes to
the bathroom, you may find yourself on more than one
occasion asking your child to hold it, only to realize he
did not make it all the way to the bathroom. If you realize
that he did wait an acceptable period of time and it may
truly be your responsibility that he did not make it to the
bathroom, it could serve you well to tell your son that you
accept responsibility for this accident. It can be a relief for
him to know that, at least this time, the accident was not

his fault. Your confession could also serve as a hands-on learning experience that nobody is perfect, a particularly valuable lesson in the midst of such a difficult feat as potty training.

Finally, if your child did ask to use the bathroom and did not manage to "hold it" for what you consider to be a reasonable period of time, now is a great opportunity to educate him about what it means to hold it and how holding it works best. As you discuss holding it, incorporate factors such as how long you should expect him to be able to hold it, what he can do to help hold his bladder, and, equally important, what *not* to do.

As you're talking to your child, begin by explaining how long he will need to hold it in terms that he will understand. For example, "We are five minutes from home. Can you hold it that long?" or "I need you to hold it for as long as it takes you to sing your ABCs three times." These statements use concepts your child will understand and also serve to divert his attention from his pressing need.

As your child continues to fight his urges, you can encourage him to think about other things in his life (toys, TV shows, etc.) that will entertain him while he waits, and you can also encourage his natural instinct to begin the "potty dance." By distracting him both mentally and physically, you are reducing the possibility of an accident while simultaneously teaching him how to hold it on his own in the future.

Finally, make sure you are pointing out to your child everything he does not want to do as he waits to find a bathroom. This is a great age to begin discouraging your child, particularly boys, from touching themselves in public. Many children feel inclined to hold their hands between their legs in an attempt to alleviate pressure, but these habits can also lead to future habits of scratching, adjusting, and other forms of contact with their genitalia that may be offensive to others.

STEP 4: TALK TO YOUR CHILD ABOUT WHAT TO DO DIFFERENTLY IN THE FUTURE.

Once you have established his answer as to why he didn't ask for a bathroom, even if he simply says, "I didn't know I needed to go," or "I forgot," you still have a starting point for the rest of your conversation. Now is the time for you to remind him of the importance of watching his bathroom habits, asking for a bathroom in the future, and avoiding messy accidents that are more associated with babies than they are with big kids. These conversations will be particularly effective if your child has younger siblings or younger friends as they will serve as one more comparison point for what he was (i.e., a baby) and what he wants to be (a big kid!).

Dripping, Leaking, and More

Another frequent problem with potty training is not outright accidents but the very real possibility that your child is experiencing leaking or dripping. This can be frustrating and confusing for many parents, but it is a normal problem that can occur in children of any age up through adulthood. There are many possible causes to leaking, and parents often find themselves solving the problem without ever realizing what was happening.

Vaginal Reflux

Females often have a problem with urine traveling into their vagina during urination. This problem is more common in toddlers and young children because female toddlers often prefer to sit with their legs closed together while using a toilet or potty chair. This position often results from the unusual feeling of peeing or pooping outside of a diaper, the insecurity of sitting on a seat with a gaping hole, or simply a desire to cover parts that are usually covered by clothing. If you find this is a problem, work on teaching your daughter to sit with her legs spread. This position will increase her overall hygiene, give her better stability on the seat, and decrease the possibility of vaginal reflux, because her open legs will help spread her labia. It may help if you demonstrate sitting like this for her (although it is not uncommon for mothers to feel uncomfortable with this level of exposure). Another possibility is to have your daughter sit on the toilet before she reaches the point of urgency, and then help her find a way to spread her legs that results in a comfortable sitting position for her that will also result in the decreased possibility of vaginal reflux. If neither of these methods works, you can also try having your daughter sit backward on the toilet. While this is not the ideal long-term solution, it will help your daughter find her balance on the toilet while she finds comfort in keeping her legs spread while she urinates.

Overactive Bladder

Like vaginal reflux, overactive bladders can affect people of all ages. Overactive bladders in toddlers are most often the result of a frequent, urgent need to use the bathroom. If your toddler experiences leaking or dripping as a result of an overactive bladder, chances are good she will not even sense the need to urinate before, during, or after the leaking itself. Most toddlers grow out of overactive bladders, but you may consider speaking to her pediatrician about further options if the problem persists as she nears her first day of school. There are drugs available to help people overcome overactive bladders, but these medicines are typically withheld unless necessary, and even then are mostly prescribed to adults with ongoing problems.

Urinary Incontinence

Urinary incontinence is the technical term for a condition when someone simply cannot hold her bladder. When dealing with incontinence in toddlers, it is first important to understand that, while it is a normal condition for people of all ages to experience, it is particularly common in toddlers who are first exploring the possibility of potty training. Incontinence typically disappears by the time toddlers reach the age of five. When a child needs to pee, the sac that stores urine (also known as the detrusor) contracts and eliminates. The sphincter muscles, which are otherwise tightened to avoid urinating, relax, thereby allowing a person to urinate. When a toddler experiences incontinence, this is either a sign that her nervous system has not yet matured enough for potty training or that she has an overactive bladder.

🅔❗ Alert

If your toddler is experiencing urinary incontinence and does not suffer from an overactive bladder, this may be another sign that she is not yet ready to begin potty training. Just as it is important for a child to be mentally prepared for the responsibility and education that comes with potty training, her body must also be ready to perform all of the functions necessary for proper potty training, including control over her sphincter muscles.

Urinary Tract Infections

Urinary tract infections, also known as UTIs, are a frequent cause of incontinence problems in women of all ages. UTIs occur when bacteria has made its way up the urethra and into the bladder. One common cause of UTIs in young girls is when they wipe back to front instead of front to back. Because urine does not normally contain bacteria, it is when bacteria is moved from one place in the genital/rectal area toward the urethra that an infection will most likely occur. Symptoms of a UTI include irritation of the urethra, bladder, or kidneys. If your child is not old enough or verbal enough to indicate these problems, you can also watch for general irritability, loss of appetite, or high fever. Visit your pediatrician if you suspect that your child may have a UTI. She may prescribe an antibiotic to help fight the infection, which will also help clear up any incontinence problems.

Preparing for Diarrhea

If your child has reached potty-training age, you have more than likely handled multiple cases of diarrhea, the loose, watery stools that typically occur at least three times per day. You have probably had your own experiences with diarrhea as well, so you are already familiar with the signs and treatment available. However, it is important to review the circumstances surrounding and solutions for diarrhea when it involves your children. Although diarrhea is most often the result of a viral infection, it usually goes away on its own. There are medications for adults to take when suffering from diarrhea, but it is best to avoid these medicines with young children. Diarrhea in children is most often associated with the rotavirus, a virus that involves rapid dehydration and high fever. Although there is a vaccine available for rotavirus, it is important to mention to your doctor if you have been traveling recently if your child comes down with a case of diarrhea. Rotavirus is particularly dangerous in third world countries where proper intravenous medications and other hydration methods are not always available. Although rotavirus is entirely treatable, it can be fatal if left unattended. In general you should treat your child's diarrhea with plenty of fluids to avoid dehydration, liquids with electrolytes such as Pedialyte, and rest to avoid fever, vomiting, or other symptoms associated with stomach illnesses.

 Fact

Although sports drinks are a good way to increase your healthy child's electrolytes, these beverages are typically too high in sugar to be beneficial while suffering from diarrhea. Typically, clear liquids are recommended for a child suffering from diarrhea, so choosing a drink specifically intended for an ill child is often the better choice (although milk is still an option).

Once you have established that your child does have diarrhea, you will need to plan accordingly for how to best prevent accidents. Given the size of the stool and the frequency with which diarrhea can occur, parents usually must deal with a sense of urgency and a possible loss of control. These problems, in addition to the newness of using a toilet rather than a diaper, can make it particularly difficult and sometimes impossible for a toddler to maintain control of his bowels.

Tips to help your child avoid having a public accident associated with diarrhea:

1. Avoid public places until the diarrhea has passed. Although you may intend to ask your child continuously and may have an extremely well-prepared bag

of supplies available in case an accident does occur, the fact remains that the majority of the responsibility for preventing a diarrhea accident lies in your toddler. At the same time, your toddler is likely fatigued from his illness, distracted by his symptoms, and still unfamiliar with the feeling of impending diarrhea.

2. Maintain hydration to help the diarrhea pass. Just as you can use fluids to help prevent further dehydration in your child, drinking plenty of liquids can also help flush your child's symptoms, thereby helping him overcome the diarrhea. You should use fluids rich in electrolytes, but many of your child's more typical beverages are also acceptable. Although adults may complain of discomfort or irritability when drinking a dairy-heavy liquid like whole or two percent milk, your child's stomach is more than likely accustomed to such a beverage as a regular part of his diet, and therefore should not experience any extra problems as a result.

3. Avoid foods that may be difficult to digest. This includes foods like yogurt or ice cream that are particularly high in dairy content, fruit juices that are too high in sugar and can also cause diarrhea, and high fiber foods. Many parents try to encourage high fiber foods when their children suffer from diarrhea in order to help bind the stool and prevent further watery bowel movements, but these binding agents can also further agitate an already irritated digestive system.

The fact of the matter is that diarrhea is rarely predictable, particularly in children who do not yet understand how to fully communicate the problems they may be having. You also may feel that your child has overcome diarrhea, only to suffer a relapse the next day. Consequently, it is important for you as the parent to be prepared for the possibility of an accident involving diarrhea.

🅴❗ Alert

Some parents may turn to diapers or training pants as a preventative measure when their child is sick. This can often lead to regression, however, as your child once again may feel it is unnecessary to use a toilet in order to pee or poop. Additionally, diapers and training pants, while good for typical urinary and bowel movements, are often incapable of holding diarrhea, so accidents will still occur.

First, you need to get past any potential embarrassment. It can be embarrassing for you and your child if he has a diarrhea accident in a public place, but while you are attempting to overcome your embarrassment, the accident remains.

After the Accident

Next, you need to accept your own responsibility for cleaning up any signs of the accident. Because diarrhea is wet and loose, chances are high that your child's accident will pass out of his clothes and onto the seat beneath him or the floor below. While there are employees who are paid to clean up their work environment, they are not paid to clean up your child's bathroom problems. This is particularly important when facing diarrhea because diarrhea is typically a sign of an illness, may be contagious, and should not be spread to the people around your child if at all possible. This does not mean that you should carry a full assortment of cleaning supplies with you just in case your child has such an accident, but you should be willing to use the cleaning agents provided by others in order to clean your own child's mess.

Once the area is cleaned, you also need to make sure you clean your child properly. This is where your handy bag of supplies for your post–potty-trained child will be most helpful. If you have taken the earlier advice of keeping extra clothes, wipes, and rash cream handy even after potty training has ended, you are well prepared for this event. Diarrhea is much like urine in its potentially high acid content, so you will want to change your child as soon as possible and as clean him as thoroughly as possible. You may want to consider using a rash cream now as a preventative measure since your child's skin has already been exposed to the acid. Finally, you will want to have a plastic bag available to contain the soiled clothes and the potentially infectious, and most likely smelly, mess that goes with them.

Conclusion

Now that you are prepared to handle accidents in a hygienic fashion and treat them as learning experiences, you are ready to venture out into the world with your potty-trained child. Be sure to maintain your supplies for a considerable period of time after your child has finished potty training. The old adage instructs you to "always expect the unexpected," and this can apply to almost any parenting situation.

CHAPTER 9

Toilet Training a Child with Special Needs

Potty training is one of toddlerhood's most significant developmental milestones. When your child is able to graduate from diapers to underwear, a new sense of independence and accomplishment will emerge. Children with disabilities (developmental, learning, physical, and behavioral) may need some adjustments to their daily schedules as well as the overall potty-training plan so that they may achieve their goal. Never assume that a child with learning disabilities or special needs will remain incontinent.

Potty-Training Readiness

It is important to take another look at the steps necessary for successful potty training so that you will have a clear map to guide you when determining the readiness of your child. The first step your child must demonstrate is the ability to feel the urge to urinate and have bowel movements. This ability is typically first seen in children between the ages of fifteen and twenty-four months. In children with special needs however, these signs may come somewhat later.

The next step involves your child mastering the ability to hold in urine or stool. Your child being able to stay dry for at least two hours may demonstrate this skill. The ability to stay dry or "hold it" is usually seen around twenty-six to twenty-nine months but again may be later for children of special needs. You may observe your child doing the potty dance, squatting down on her heels, or standing very still with her buttocks squeezed together. This can be frustrating for parents who mistake these cues as attempts to avoid going to the potty. On the contrary, when these behaviors are observed, parents should be encouraged that their little one has the ability to hold urine or stool.

Now it is time to identify your child's ability to communicate, since communication between the two of you during potty training is essential to your success. The good news is that this communication may be in the form of both words and gestures. As long as you and your child have some way to exchange information, you are ready to move to the next step. This becomes very important in helping your child be successful when she is using a potty in a new or different environment.

The next step is to ensure that your child can get to the potty with minimal assistance. She must then be able to pull down her pants and underwear and sit on the potty (seat or chair). The ability to sit on the toilet usually occurs around twenty-six to thirty-one months of age. In children of special needs, this may occur at a later age. Once on the toilet or potty chair, your child must relax and either urinate or defecate. She will not be able to have a bowel movement if she is unable to relax. Focus on the posture your child assumes on the potty, because this is related to her ability to relax. Remember, a step-stool may be necessary for children who are too short to reach the floor with their feet.

Invariably your child will choose just the wrong time to head off to the potty to poop. It is important for her to not feel rushed or hurried as she goes during training (this may carry over beyond the training period). Some experts recommend having your child practice sitting on the potty and relaxing when she doesn't have use it. Having your child practice this about thirty minutes after a meal can be very helpful since the body's natural reflex (called the gastrocolic reflex) is to defecate or poop. Some parents choose to help children relax by sitting with them and reading a book or singing a song. This is not the time to rough house though. You may wish to demonstrate relaxation by closing your eyes and taking a couple of deep breaths. In order to get to the next step of peeing or pooping, you may wish to have your child blow bubbles to stimulate the Valsalva maneuver.

 Fact

> The Valsalva maneuver or response is that feeling you have when bearing down. This may be difficult to communicate to a child with special needs, so seeking alternate ways to elicit the response is often necessary. Holding a tissue in front of the child and asking her to blow is an option. Blowing on a toy horn is another option.

Next, the child must also be able to wipe, get off the potty, pull up her pants, flush the potty, and wash her hands. Wiping is a skill that is not easily learned for most children. Your child must have fine motor skills and coordination. Even after the training process, you will likely need to work with her to refine the skill and ensure cleanliness. Once she has mastered wiping, she will be ready to pull up her pants, flush the potty, and wash her hands.

These steps are simple and effective and can be used whether or not your child has special needs. Assisting your child through these steps is a clear and concise approach to toilet training. When she masters each step, she affirms her abilities and reassures you that you both have made progress. You may wish to use some sort of system to reward your child for making progress. As previously discussed, stickers, small toys, and books are some examples of rewards. Remember, rewarding your child with food or candy is an unhealthy habit to begin. It is important that you begin now reinforcing good behavior and accomplishments with things other than food so that healthy habits can be established.

You may be thinking that toilet training your child is a monumental task, especially when learning difficulties are involved. Do not be discouraged; the steps that have been discussed are merely modified for special needs. You may want to take a look at the readiness criteria discussed in previous chapters in order to determine your child's physiological age. In other words, your child may be four years old by the calendar but developmentally behaves more in line with a two year old. Her physiological age would therefore be two years old. This is extremely helpful for you and other caregivers as you can adjust what to expect from your child and minimize the potential frustrations that may occur when tasks are not accomplished.

Potty Training the Child with ADHD

Attention-deficit/hyperactivity disorder (ADHD) is a neurological disease that is found in 4 to 7 percent of children and affects boys more often than girls. Children are not typically diagnosed with this condition until after they have reached school age. In order to arrive at this diagnosis, children must meet several criteria. Symptoms must be present in more than one setting (e.g., home and school), observed prior to age seven, and must contribute to deficits in school work, the accomplishment of tasks, and an overall impairment of performance. Other disorders or conditions frequently coexist with ADHD, including depression, anxiety disorder, oppositional defiant disorder, and tics. Although the diagnosis of ADHD is not usually made until the school age years, some children my show symptoms while they are still preschool age. ADHD presents differently for each child; some children may show only mild inattention while others are extremely inattentive and have the hyperactive component as well.

Essential

If you think your child might have ADHD, be on the lookout for symptoms such as making careless mistakes, not listening when spoken to, avoiding tasks with which she is unfamiliar, and not paying attention to details. The hyperactive symptoms include fidgeting, climbing, running excessively, difficulty waiting for her turn, interrupting conversations, and difficulty playing quietly.

Many of the symptoms of ADHD (fidgeting, climbing, running excessively, and difficulty waiting for her turn) are seen in children in the preschool years and are considered to be normal for this age. Thus, it is important that parents discuss their concerns with health care providers in order to determine whether or not their child's behavior is normal for her developmental age. In fact, many of these symptoms persist through the early school age years (kindergarten and first grade), with boys typically showing more symptoms than girls. If you are concerned about inattentive behavior in your child, consult your health care provider. She can help you evaluate whether or not sending your child to kindergarten is a good idea. This becomes especially important if your child has a "late" birthday or is on the younger side of five years old. Again, discussing your child's behavior during well-child exams is a great way to gain more information that will help you determine potty-training readiness as well as readiness for school.

As you may expect, training a child with a limited attention span and focus can be a challenge. If you have been diligently working to potty train your five-year-old who refuses to sit on the potty, you may want to consider whether or not she is showing early signs and symptoms of ADHD. Children who have ADHD often have difficulty switching their focus from one activity to another. This is clearly a problem as these children struggle with acknowledging the urge to use the potty, getting to the potty, and sitting on the potty long enough to relax and urinate or have a bowel movement. Children with an attention deficit may have significant difficulty in stopping a preferred activity in order to attend to basic needs like eating or using the toilet, so it is no surprise that they may also have difficulty sitting down long enough to have a complete bowel movement.

Helping Your Child with ADHD

If you have been struggling with the "final" phase of potty training with an older toddler, it is important to consider whether or not your child has one of the comorbid conditions (conditions occurring at the same time) mentioned previously. A refusal to use the toilet or your child's inability to carry out the steps you've been working on may be partially attributed to oppositional defiance or anxiety along with an attention deficit. Although you may become very frustrated with your child when she refuses to use the potty, your emotions must remain neutral. Children with oppositional defiance or anxiety disorders will only worsen if parents show outward signs of anger, frustration, and stress. Treat accidents lightly. In addition, remember to go at your child's pace when potty training. Be sure to give encouragement and praise for each success. You can also prevent or reduce your child's anxiety by beginning potty training at a time of low stress. Avoid times of change such as with the birth of a new baby, a divorce, or a move to a new home. If you find yourself already in the middle of training and are now realizing the impact a life change or stressor has had on your child, it is always okay to abandon efforts for now and resume once family routines become normalized.

There are other things that may be helpful for use in children whose ADHD has prevented successful attempts at toilet training. Begin by watching videos or reading books about potty training. Choose short videos for your child, and ones with a character she likes so that her attention will be captured. Create a structured environment, as children with ADHD tend to respond positively to routines. Another way to ensure your child sticks to a routine is by using scheduled toilet times. Experts recommend using a watch that you can set to beep at intervals (two hours is typically appropriate), thereby alerting your child to stop her activity and take a bathroom break. This alarm may also serve as a neutral party that keeps the parent from being the "bad guy" repeatedly during the training process. In other words, the beep is the audible reminder that the parent would otherwise need to give every two hours. Another suggestion is to reduce your expectations of your child's attention span since this is clearly a challenge for children with ADHD. This is primarily done by decreasing the amount of time your child must sit on the potty. If your child is older, however, you may wish to try using handheld computers or games to divert her attention from the task at hand. If you're using a reward system, you must issue the reward immediately following mastery of the potty-training step(s). If you have concerns that your child's potty-training process is not going according to plan, contact your health care provider to discuss a referral to a behavioral therapist or other child development specialist.

Potty Training Children with Autism Spectrum Disorders

Asperger's syndrome and autism spectrum disorders belong to a group of ailments known as pervasive developmental disorders (PDD). Autism spectrum disorders affect between 1 in 80 and 1 in 240 children in the United States, according to the Centers for Disease Control. The disorders cross all racial, ethnic, and socioeconomic groups, and affect boys almost five times more often than girls.

Asperger's syndrome is considered to be on the lower end of the autism spectrum. Children with Asperger's have difficulty interacting with other people and making friends. In other words, these children have some of the same characteristics as children with autism. They have difficulty with change and clearly prefer routine. However, unlike children with autism, those with Asperger's syndrome do not typically experience language delays; they begin to speak before the age of two years. The diagnosis is usually noticed around age three or later. The exact cause of Asperger's is unknown, but there appears to be a genetic link as it tends to run in families. A diagnosis of Asperger's syndrome is made when there has been no history of delays in language or cognition.

 Fact

Children with Asperger's have a hard time relating to others. They are not able to express their feelings, so temper tantrums are common. They have difficulty recognizing verbal and nonverbal cues. They may be bothered by loud noises, lights, and different textures. They often focus intensely on only one or two things, like an unusual interest in alligators or types of squash.

Children with autism tend to have more severe symptoms. Sometimes their development is delayed from birth, while others develop on schedule but suddenly lose language skills. These children also have difficulty learning language overall. They make little eye contact and do not like to be picked up or cuddled. They have difficulty relating to the feelings of other children and therefore do not play with children or make friends easily. You may see repetitive movements such as hand flapping, rocking, or pacing in some children with autism. Children with autism will often use big words without knowing their meaning. They tend to tune out their surroundings, so they can seem sensitive to certain sounds despite the frequent appearance of being deaf.

Challenges for Training

Recent surveys of parents of children with autism show more than 50 percent reporting problems with potty training. Further reports indicate that approximately 11 percent have urinary accidents while almost 7 percent have stooling accidents. The problems faced by children with autism are more often related to the struggles caused by them being unable to perform developmentally appropriate tasks at their chronological age. Due to language delays and challenges with communication, children with autism may have difficulty understanding instructions and verbalizing the need to go to the potty.

One of the other challenges many children with autism face is that of unpredictable bowel habits. Gastrointestinal problems, including loose or hard stools, may cause some difficulty for parents and children as they work toward successful potty training. As discussed in earlier chapters, it is necessary to regulate bowel movements so that your child does not experience painful potty experiences. Another complicating factor for children with autism is the different potty-related sensations they experience. Some children seek out certain sensory behaviors such as rubbing the corner of a favorite satin blanket, while others work to avoid sensations. Therefore children may not feel the urge to go potty or may resist going completely if they do feel the urge. Constipation must be managed using laxatives or fiber agents to keep stools soft and "routine" for children with autism. Likewise, it is important to use bulking agents or stool thickening foods to help children with diarrhea form more solid stools that can be controlled. Probiotics are an option for children with both diarrhea and constipation as they regulate bowel function and restore its ability to absorb nutrients and regulate water absorption in the bowel.

In addition to the above challenges, children with autism spectrum disorders are similar to children with ADHD in that they have difficulty changing activities. Recognizing the urge or sensation of needing to potty is only part of the challenge. Your child must then leave the activity they are engaged in and get there. Unfortunately, children with autism spectrum disorders do not shift gears as easily and are therefore more at risk for having accidents. Some experts recommend prompted voiding or scheduled toilet times as a way to prevent accidents. However, over time it is also recommended that you remove these prompts so that your child learns to initiate going to the potty independently. Remember, regardless of his older age, your child's developmental task is to become autonomous or independent in self care.

SHANNON, Mother of Jem, age 6:

"My son Jem has autism, so we had help with potty training. Our therapists set up a schedule that started with giving him a drink and then setting a timer for ten minutes. When the timer went off, my husband, the therapist, and I would all act like it was a big party. We would dance, sing the potty song, and have races to the bathroom. We would put Jem on the potty chair and clap, and then either my husband or I would sit and read to him. The therapist would set the timer for five minutes and Jem would sit on the potty for the entire time. If he happened to pee during those five minutes, we would act like it was an even bigger party and shower him with praise, singing, and dancing. If he didn't pee, he would come off the toilet and the timer would be reset for five minutes, and we would repeat until he either peed in the potty (big party) or peed in his pants (with no reaction from us). We would very quietly and kindly change his soiled pants, but there would be no recriminations or scolding as well as no hugs and kisses—just a nonreaction. It took three days for him to get it and two weeks to perfect it. It meant we didn't go out a lot in those two weeks, but it worked."

Helping Your Child with Autism Spectrum Disorders

One way to minimize the challenges of potty training a child with autism spectrum disorders is by choosing a method that suits your child's developmental abilities. By this point, it is likely that you have invested a good deal of time establishing your child's readiness. For example, you have spent time with your child choosing a potty seat or chair that he is likely to really use. It is possible that a child with autism will require additional help as you begin to go through the steps of potty training due to his struggles with communication. One system that you may find beneficial for giving visual cues to your child is the Picture Exchange Communication System. This system includes several drawings that are used to educate children with autism. In addition, once you begin the toilet training process, you will want to include his teachers or caregivers in the plan since they will be able to provide the toileting prompts and reinforcements during the day. It is important to remember that you are not alone in the process of toilet training your child with autism spectrum disorder. Several parenting websites are available with blogs that provide not only up-to-the-minute posts, but also archived posts that can be helpful for parents facing challenges. Further, your child's healthcare provider may be able to provide referrals to behavioral therapists specializing in children with special needs.

Children with autism may require added motivation to sit on the potty. Sometimes the motivation may be the reward for having a successful potty time. Parents may decide to allow their child to hold a favorite toy or read a favorite story (more than once) in order to keep the child's attention diverted from the act of pooping. Sometimes parents may choose to allow the motivational toy or movie to be played with only when he is in the bathroom. This should keep his interest for the time necessary to master the acts of peeing and pooping. Remember, using the experience and expertise of other parents and therapists may save you and your child much frustration during the potty-training process.

SHANNON, mother of Jem, 6:

"Jem was terrified to poop in the potty. We tried the same tactics we had tried with peeing, but with little success. He would get off the toilet and then poop. While on the potty, he would actually hold it so that he could wait to go after getting off the potty. We did a few different things to help Jem get over this hurdle. First, we modeled it for him. It's gross, I know, but he saw mom and dad sitting on the toilet, and then we showed him our poop in the toilet and that seemed to register. We started feeding him a pear in the morning and then waiting an hour and putting him on the potty for ten minutes at a time. To keep him there, we gave him a portable DVD player loaded with his favorite cartoons. That worked occasionally and started getting him over his fear of pooping in the potty, but he still couldn't get the sensation down and link it up with going into the bathroom. Finally, we resorted to bribery, and it worked like gangbusters. We took him to the toy store and let him pick out a toy. He happened to pick a LEGO knight. We took it home and put it on the shelf in the bathroom where he could see it and told him he couldn't have it until he pooped in the potty. He didn't believe us at first and cried that he wanted the toy. Once he realized that we meant business, he sat down and pooped. We instantly gave him the toy. That night when he went to bed, the toy went back on the shelf. When he got up in the morning, he asked for it. We repeated the process. We told him that as soon as he pooped in the potty, he could have the toy. We did that for months. If he had an accident, we never yelled, but he wasn't allowed to play with it until he pooped. We periodically bought more LEGO Knights to sweeten the pot (no pun intended) and it kept him interested. I've told several other moms the trick with the toy on the shelf, and they have all had great results."

Potty Training Children with Sensory Integration Dysfunction

Sensory integration dysfunction, also known as sensory processing disorder, is a diagnosis that refers to a glitch in the system of taking in stimulus, processing it, and responding to it. Sensory integration begins before birth and continues throughout life. However, the most important development occurs before a child reaches the age of seven. When a sensory processing system is working according to plan, the neurological system (sight, sound, taste, touch, and smell) receives a message, the brain sorts and filters the message, and the body or person uses the information to adapt to the environment. Adapting to the environment is how children develop "normally." In addition to the five main senses, humans also have six other senses. These are the sense of time, nociception (pain), proprioception (joint motion), equilibrioception (balance), thermoception (temperature), magnetoception (direction), and interoception (internal senses). This system works without the need for any conscious prompting by the child. The adaptations help children (and adults) learn how to navigate their environment socially (communication with others), physically (motor development), and mentally (focus and attention).

It is important to note that sensory processing is not a destination, but rather a journey that one travels over time. Everyone has problems with certain stimuli (examples include fingernails on a chalkboard, biting into a popsicle, or firecrackers), but sensory perception is considered to be a problem only when there are extreme reactions. Sensory processing disorder is diagnosed when children react to sensory input differently than others. It is a neurological problem, and, although some of the symptoms are similar to that of autism spectrum disorders and ADHD, sensory processing disorder is not the same as any of these even though it may accompany any of them.

Some of the more common sensory processing challenges seen in children are the inability to tolerate the tag in a shirt, the need for the seam of a sock to be perfectly straight across the toes, over-reaction to noises like vacuum cleaners or airplanes, and food textural aversion.

Children with sensory processing disorders are a challenge in many ways. From the perspective of the health care provider, these children are a challenge as there is no distinct disorder or medical model that totally explains the disorder. In addition to the five main senses, children with sensory processing disorder have challenges with interoceptive senses, or those senses that typically are stimulated from within the body that require no conscious effort on the child's part. Some examples of interoceptive senses include pulmonary stretch receptors that help regulate breathing rates, stretch receptors in the bladder and bowel that give the sense of fullness or need to empty, receptors in the pharynx that cause a child to gag from certain foods or textures, and receptors in the skin that cause blood vessels to dilate and create blushing cheeks. It is easy to see, therefore, how a child with sensory processing disorder will likely have difficulty with potty training.

A child with sensory processing disorder will often not feel the urge to empty her bowel or bladder. If she does feel the urge, it is possible that the interoceptive system is not picking up or interpreting the message properly. In other words, your child may not even know she needs to use the bathroom and, if she does, she doesn't know how to control the muscles regulating her bowel and bladder. Specifically, the deficit in sensory processing may show up as your child rushes to the potty at the last minute only to be too late. It may be seen as your child sits for long periods of time on the potty with no results. These children may suffer from constipation or painful bowel movements. Older children with sensory processing disorders may become frustrated or ashamed by frequent accidents or the need to continue to use disposable training pants or diapers. They may, however, feel the sensation but become overwhelmed by it and then become confused or flustered as they attempt to respond to the urge in a logical fashion. Even the seemingly simple task of wiping can be overwhelming for a child with sensory integration disorder.

Helping Your Child with Sensory Integration Disorder

It is important for you to recognize the symptoms of sensory processing disorder so that you may create an environment that will minimize the frustration or anxiety related to potty training. As a parent, you must first understand that your potty-training experiences with this child will be markedly different than those experiences with unaffected children and those of your peers. It is crucial to wait until your child's developmental age is appropriate for potty training. Remember, her chronological age is not relevant here. Experts recommend using a child-oriented approach when potty training a child with sensory processing disorder.

Once you have determined your child's readiness (physiological and psychological), you should spend a minimum of three months preparing her for potty training. During the preparation phase, allow your child to help choose a potty chair or potty seat. Create a basket of potty-time goodies including toilet paper, wipes, a book, aroma therapy spray, a reward chart, and music your child enjoys, and proceed just as you would in other child-oriented methods. Be sure to watch your child's expressions while she practices sitting on the potty. If you feel she has had a result, ask her if she felt it. Help her sort out how she feels following peeing and pooping. This is a good way to help your child learn the cues. Another suggestion is to have your child place her hand on the lower part of his tummy to gain a sense of coordinating the sensations of the tummy feeling full and firm while pooping. Create an environment where your child can feel comfortable and calm.

You may also need to remove items, like clutter or decorations, from the bathroom that distract your child from the task at hand. Remember, odors may be particularly offensive to a child with sensory processing disorder, so it may be necessary to create an environment that masks smells. If your child is using regular panties or underwear, be sure to notice how she seems to react to the underwear seams. If the seams are bothersome to the child, a parent may misinterpret her not wanting to wear that particular underwear with not wanting to potty train. You will want to take things slowly if your child is potty trained for peeing but not pooping. Again moving at the child's pace, slowly encourage her to sit on the potty with her diaper on to have a bowel movement. Once she's done it, dump the stool into the potty and allow her to flush it. Make up a silly song, wave, and praise your child as she flushes.

You may need to make peeing fun, so add food coloring to the toilet bowl. Adding blue to the water will create green when your child urinates successfully. You may also wish to create targets in the toilet bowl that encourage your child to "aim" for success just as parents of neurotypical children use.

e★ Essential

Like other steps of development, you will most likely find yourself using many of the same methods in potty training your special needs child that parents of neurotypical children use; the only difference is that you may need to be prepared for the process to take longer, to use more methods, and to encounter more frustration both in yourself and your child.

Above all, avoid punishing your child with sensory integration disorders during the potty-training process.

She needs to know that you will support her as she struggles to master this developmental task. Teaching relaxation techniques such as deep breathing and positive imagery are helpful in decreasing the anxiety your child may feel as the process continues. And, just as suggested for children with ADHD and autism spectrum disorders, using a behavioral therapist or occupational therapist is an excellent way to draw from the experiences of others to create a successful outcome for you and your child.

Potty Training Children with Physical Disabilities

Children with physical disabilities are frequently slower to potty train than children without physical limitations. Sometimes this may be due to accompanying learning disabilities that prevent them from understanding or remembering the steps to going to the potty. They may have difficulty sensing bowel and bladder fullness or the urge to potty. In addition, they may have difficulty with the physical act of getting to the potty, pulling down their pants, sitting on the potty, and wiping. And lastly, they may have difficulty communicating the need to potty.

When a physical disability of the lower body is present, a child's ability to walk and engage in activity is limited and muscle tone is diminished. This decreased activity level and muscle tone can contribute to problems with constipation and, as discussed in previous chapters, constipation brings its own challenges to the potty-training process. In addition, some children may have atypical posture that makes emptying the bowel and bladder more difficult. Upper body limitations may prevent your child from being able to balance on the commode and wipe after they have gone successfully. Muscle tone and control are extremely important as you move forward in potty training your child with physical disabilities.

Before beginning the potty-training process in a child with physical disabilities, it is important that you discuss your plans with your child's health care provider. She can help you determine your child's readiness to potty train. In addition, you can discuss any limitations that may impact overall continence. For example, children with spina bifida may have complete incontinence of bowel and bladder, or they may have only mild symptoms of neurogenic bowel and bladder that requires minimal modification. It is also important to determine whether or not your child has any pain while peeing or pooping. It is possible that he will begin to withhold stool if he is in pain with pooping, thereby creating a vicious cycle of pain, withholding, constipation, pain, etc. If your child is constipated, you will need to find a way to soften his stools. This can be done with dietary measures as discussed in Chapter 5 or with medication. Stool softeners or laxatives should not be used without first consulting your child's health care provider, as many are formulated for adult usage and can have dangerous side effects in children when not used according to physician recommendations.

Readiness for potty training in a child with physical disabilities is determined similarly to a child without physical disabilities. However, a few additions to the checklist must be made. In determining your child's readiness, ask yourself the following questions: can he sit with minimal or no support? Does he try to squat without losing his balance? Can he walk without help? Does he have upper body strength? Does he have manual dexterity needed to wipe? Does he have the ability to communicate the need to pee or poop? Does he stay dry for extended periods of time? Does he have soft, formed bowel movements? Once you have completed the readiness checklist with the addition of the above items, it is a good idea to keep a voiding diary for three to five days. Make notes in the diary that include each time your child has a drink and is wet along with each time your child eats and has a bowel movement. Remember, it is not a good idea to begin potty training if your family is in a stressful time such as a move, bringing home a new baby, changing schools, and divorce.

Motivating your child with physical disabilities is really no different than motivating a child without physical disabilities. Hugs, praise, and small toys or trinkets are often effective methods for getting your child to perform the potty-training task at hand. And, just as with all children, punishment for accidents (that are certain to occur) is not an option.

Helping Your Child with Physical Disabilities

It is important to assess the physical aspect of how your child sits on the potty. If upper body strength or posture is a problem, a parent may need to sit with the child to help stabilize him while he uses the potty. However, if upper body strength is not an issue and/or modifications such as grab bars have already been installed, parental presence is not necessary. This further promotes your child's progress toward independence.

 Fact

An occupational therapist is an invaluable resource for parents of children with physical disabilities. They are well-versed in adapting environments to meet the needs of children with physical limitations.

Raised toilet seats and safety bars are a nice option for children who are older and taller. For toddlers, however, several potty chairs are commercially available with backs that support posture. Sometimes, just having your child sit differently on the potty will help with challenging postures. Having your child sit backward on the potty holding the lid or tank may help, while sitting sideways and using the wall to balance is another option. If your child needs more extensive support while on the potty, full systems are available that provide modification to any standard commode. For children who use wheelchairs, you may purchase wheelchair conversion products to assist your child in getting to the potty with ease and independence. If your child does not like the feel of the potty seat, you may wish to pad the seat with foam to make it more comfortable.

Potty Training Children with Mental Retardation and Down Syndrome

Children who have an intelligence quotient (IQ) less than 70 and have an impaired ability to function are considered to have mental retardation. Children with Down syndrome often fall into this category as well. A diagnosis of mental retardation or global developmental delay will be given to preschool age children when they consistently fail to meet developmental milestones at the projected chronological ages. The milestones are usually met in order but at a rate slower than their peers. Children with an IQ of 70 may expect to potty train around age three while children with an IQ of 50 may be closer to the age of four before potty training.

Communication and motor skills are the same for children with mental retardation as with children without mental retardation. The biggest difference lies in the need for breaking the process into smaller parts so that the child with mental retardation can grasp the concepts. Visual cues or reminders may also be helpful for use in children with mental retardation. It is important that all caregivers, teachers, and day care providers have the same visual cues and routines so that the child has consistency between settings.

For children with Down syndrome, not only is mental retardation a challenge but so is decreased muscle tone, or hypotonia. This condition is a challenge for children with Down syndrome because it makes it difficult for them to push stool out of the body. Thus, these children are frequently constipated, and you know well the challenges this brings to the process. So, for children with Down syndrome, it is important to ensure a healthy diet, including five to eight servings of fresh fruits and vegetables, whole grains, and adequate fiber. In addition, helping your child with Down syndrome recognize body responses is important. You may wish to employ techniques similar to those used for children with sensory integration disorder, in particular the method that has them place a hand on the lower abdomen to feel the muscle protrude as they "bear down" to poop.

e✔ Fact

Children with mental retardation must be evaluated from a developmental age instead of a chronological age when determining readiness for toilet training.

Smearing

Children with mental retardation and autism spectrum disorders may display a behavior known as smearing. Smearing is just as you may imagine—the child smears stool on herself, creating a feeling of satisfaction (for the child, of course). Some children engage in this behavior as an attention seeking act, while others smear to express their agitation. Some children merely do it out of boredom. Most often, children who smear stool are unaware of how unacceptable the activity is in the social setting.

It is important that parents and caregivers avoid reacting to stool smearing because it is quite likely that even a negative reaction will somehow encourage the child to do it again. Some parents report that keeping bowel movements on a schedule provides a way to change a diaper immediately following a bowel movement so that smearing can be avoided. As frustrated as you may be, it is important to determine what motivates your child to smear stool. If you can replace the activity with something that is equally satisfying, you may be able to stop it. As always, do not hesitate to contact a behavioral therapist. She will likely be able to give helpful pointers or interventions to end the activity once and for all.

Helping Your Child with Mental Retardation

Helping the child with Down syndrome and mental retardation is centered on improving communication. If verbal communication is a problem for your child, it will be important that you devise an alternate way to communicate. Hand signals or pointing to a picture are potential solutions. Remember, each caregiver, teacher and day care worker must know the signal or have the same picture in order to be consistent in the training process. It is paramount that you remain patient as you embark on the potty-training journey. Keep a positive attitude. Praise children for good behavior and, although it is difficult, try to avoid acknowledging negative behavior. If you have an older child who is able to stand, you may want to allow her to stand to be changed instead of requiring that she lay down. Above all else, keep the mood of your home (especially the bathroom) lighthearted. This will help decrease anxiety and hopefully improve your child's success with this developmental milestone.

Summary

Potty training the child with special needs is remarkably similar to potty training a child with no disabilities. You must first begin with a readiness assessment using your child's developmental age instead of his chronological age. Once you have determined your child's developmental age, you must then determine the method of potty training that best suits his needs and abilities. If your child has physical disabilities, you should invest in safety equipment (grab bars, modified toilet seats) that can be obtained and installed as necessary so that he can learn with these adaptive devices from day one. Next, you must choose a time to begin, being careful to avoid times of increased stress.

Once you have begun the training process, it is never too late to reevaluate your plan. If you begin and find yourself four weeks into a program with absolutely no progress, it is perfectly reasonable to seek outside help. Find a behavioral therapist. Talk to your child's health care provider. Contact a local children's hospital and seek out the Child Life department or the occupational therapy department for expert advice. Remember, before you become frustrated and angry, give yourself a break and call for backup. You and your child can do this!

CHAPTER 10

Becoming a Big Kid

Congratulations! You have officially reached the end of your potty-training guide and are now enjoying the wonderful world of a diaper-free child. As you leave your house with a lighter bag and the grocery store with a significantly smaller bill, there are still a few key concepts to keep in mind. Even after potty training has ended there will still be a variety of bathroom experiences that will be new and strange to your child. For example, just how different are the bathrooms outside your house? Why are some bathrooms only for boys and some bathrooms only for girls? What if he just can't hold it any longer? You as a parent will also have questions. What do you do as a mother when your son seems too old for a women's bathroom? What should a father do when his daughter seems too old for a men's room? When, if ever, is it appropriate to revert to a diaper? This chapter will focus on answering all of these questions, and more, in order to best send you off into the world as the parent of a diaper-free child.

When You Aren't at Home

If you have made it this far and already started potty training your child, you have likely begun to notice many of the following situations. First, your child has probably expressed a fascination with public restrooms. Particularly if you visit the same store repeatedly (such as your grocery store or pharmacy), your child has likely learned where the bathrooms are and asks to use them each time you pass. She may be asking because she genuinely needs to go, or she may just be asking because she is interested in going into this new and fascinating location within the store. Although you may be tempted to ask her to hold it till she gets home, either because you do not like public restrooms or because you realize the likelihood that she really does need to use the bathroom is low, it is in you and your child's best interests to overcome this temptation. The fact of the matter is that she is asking to go to the bathroom, and that is a good sign. For your own sake, it is better to take the extra five or ten minutes to go into the bathroom and wait for her potential elimination than to accidentally teach her that asking to go to the bathroom is a futile effort. Even if she originally asked to go to the bathroom out of sheer curiosity, you may both be surprised to learn that the need was genuine once she finds herself on a toilet.

Using a public restroom can be a giant hurdle to overcome for children as well as parents. For some children this is no big deal. For some parents this is a giant issue. For some children going into the big, mommy-size bathroom is fun. For some parents the idea of needing to take their little cherub into a public restroom is disgusting. Children are very perceptive; even though your child has never heard you say how much you dislike public restrooms, she picks up on your nonverbal cues or body language each time you enter one. If she has heard you speak negatively about public restrooms, she is likely to adopt your opinions as well. This can create further challenges as you attempt to help your child avoid accidents. If you have been guilty of this, don't worry. You can reverse the effects by changing your opinion, or at the very least faking it. Talk about the positive things you see in the potty, like how big it is, how clean it is, how it smells, or how it is decorated. You get the idea; this may be a stretch but it is also necessary if you want your child to get past her phobia.

Easing Your Child's Fears

Parents can ease their toddler's fears by using a few strategies for public potties. One is to use your own equipment. You can purchase a fold-up adapter or potty ring that easily fits in a large purse, backpack, or diaper bag. Using the adapter will help your child feel more secure as he sits on the larger potty. Another fear in a public restroom is the noise of the flush, especially since most public toilets flush with more force than do private commodes. Prepare your child ahead of time so that he knows how loud it will be. You may want to wait to flush the potty until after your child has gotten off the seat, wiped, and pulled up his pants. Some children may need to be held the first few times while the parent flushes the potty so they feel safe. Another thing to consider is the automatic flush mechanism that can be found in many commercial restrooms. The automatic flush is motion sensitive, so the commode will likely flush each time your child fidgets or sways from side to side as he sings his favorite potty song. This can be very scary for some children; they hear the noise and, because they are still seated, they feel the water spray their skin. You may need to coach your child through this process so that the flush only occurs when he moves off of the toilet seat.

Some children are so excited to use the restroom that they cannot go once seated. It is extremely frustrating for the parent who has rushed to the public potty, leaving her groceries in the middle of the shopping trip, only to have her little darling dribble out a teaspoon of urine. Be patient. He may go a little more if you allow him to sit a bit longer. If he doesn't fully empty his bladder it is a sure thing that he will need to go again either before you leave the store or at the next stop. Help your child relax on the potty by diverting his attention. Talk about the errands you are going to run that day. Ask about a friend at school. Talk about a funny part in a favorite movie or TV show. These are just a few things you can do to help him relax and empty.

Some children just have a hard time using a potty in public setting. If this is the case for your child, you may be able to help by taking him with you as you use the potty. He does not need to "try" to go or even go in the stall.

After a while, he will see that you are comfortable in the restroom and that it is not such a scary place.

The next step in using the bathroom is looking out for your child's hygiene. If you are involved in potty training, your child is probably also involved in picking his nose, possibly eating what he finds there, playing with bugs, rolling in dirt, and a whole host of other activities which he will more than likely find distasteful as he grows older. Using public restrooms is no different. His instinct will be to explore, and so he will feel comfortable grabbing the toilet, sitting on the toilet without any protective cover, reaching into the toilet if he drops something, sitting on the floor if the desire presents itself, and generally touching everything that peaks his curiosity with his bare hands. For your own sanity, it is best to find ways to compromise with his curiosity. For example, you absolutely need to teach him not to reach into the toilet, in public or anywhere else. However, it may be too soon to teach him not to touch anything. Instead, invest your own time and energy in making sure he is properly cleaned after he has finished his restroom explorations.

You also cannot change his desire to use a public bathroom, but you can use the tried-and-true "cover the seat" method your mother likely taught you when you were a child. Many public venues now provide their own seat covers, and you can also buy ready-made paper seat covers in most drug stores. However, the grassroots method of using toilet paper to cover the seat works just as well as a pre-prepared cover. This also encourages your child to learn his own way to cover the seat before he goes to the bathroom.

🅔❗ Alert

While soap and water are a good start, you may also want to carry around an antibacterial cleanser of your own. Antibacterial cleansers should be used in addition to, and not instead of, traditional soap and water methods. The soap and water will be the standard cleaning habit your child will need to adopt for all bathrooms, so do not replace washing his hands in the sink with washing his hands with your antibacterial disinfectant.

The Opposite Gender Bathroom

As your child uses a public restroom more and more, you will develop your own methods for hygiene and timing. At the same time, your child will be growing older, and this means you will be nearing an age when it is no longer appropriate to take a boy into a women's restroom and vice versa. There are several important factors to consider, however, before you decide when your child cannot come into the bathroom with you.

1. **Stranger Danger—** Although propriety is an important factor in society at any age, your child's safety trumps any person's preference for propriety. It is not worth risking your child's safety against abduc-

tion or assault of any kind just to ensure the other people in the bathroom are comfortable. Obviously, you as the adult should only use the restroom designated for your gender but, until your child has reached a safe age to use the bathroom by herself, it is your right as her parent and her right as your child to use the restroom with you. More businesses are developing family restrooms to alleviate this problem, but boys will use women's restrooms and girls will use men's restrooms when a family restroom is not available.

2. **Available Supplies**— Although society has an increasing number of single fathers and fathers as primary caregivers, the fact of the matter is that many public restrooms do not yet have changing tables available in men's rooms. In a perfect world, your child is already potty trained and this is a nonissue. However, reality dictates that children often need diapers changed even after they have indicated their need to use a restroom. Larger department stores and larger public venues such as malls are most likely to have changing facilities available for men, but it is worth your time to ask an employee before heading to a restroom with your child and being disappointed by what you do (or do not) find.

3. **Parental Comfort** — As a parent, you may not feel comfortable taking your child into a public restroom with multiple facilities available. Although this seems to be more true of men taking little girls into public restrooms, there is no one rule

for what will or will not be comfortable for parents. If you know you do not want to take your child into a public restroom with multiple facilities with you, you may want to avoid taking your child out for more than an hour at a time until you have finished potty training. You may also want to do research ahead of time to learn what venues in your area have designated family facilities. How you choose to handle your own comfort is up to you, but it is your responsibility as the parent to make sure you are prepared for the possibility that your child will need to use the bathroom in a situation that will be less than ideal for you.

KENN, Uncle of Morgan, Shelby, Barrett, and Erin
"While traveling with my sister and her family, which includes two young daughters, we visited several theme parks in California. My sister, her husband, and their oldest daughter wanted to ride a rollercoaster together at the end of the day, and I volunteered to watch their youngest daughter who was in the midst of potty training. You guessed it! She needed to go potty, "right now, Uncle Kenny!" So, reluctantly I took her into the men's restroom. I was very uncomfortable. Luckily, I was able to shuttle her into the stall quickly so she did not see anything inappropriate. However, after she finished I decided I should quickly go as well. And with a shrill, female, toddler voice, she announced, "Hey Uncle Kenny, you have your big girl panties on!" So much for getting in and out unscathed . . ."

Taking your opposite-sex child to a public restroom is a natural and necessary thing. It is really no big deal taking your toddler boy into a girl's restroom in public. He is in a private stall (as is every other patron). He is with his mom, grandma, or other female caregiver. And, more importantly, he is usually under the age of five (not eighteen). It is not like he is going to be lurking in the corner with dark glasses and a trench coat. Now, by the same token, you must teach your child how to behave in the restroom. This is necessary so that he will know the rules when he is old enough to go alone.

Restroom Manners

Although it may be funny the first time, a toddler peeking under a stall is inappropriate behavior. You must teach your child that the doors on the stalls are meant for privacy. In other words, the person behind the door does not want others to watch her potty. If your toddler is in the stall with you as you use the toilet, you may need to help preoccupy him while he waits for you to finish by telling a story, singing a song or playing pat-a-cake. Some of the newer restrooms have toddler seats installed on the back of the stall door, allowing you to strap your little one in place while you use the restroom. This is a great way to keep your little one off the floor of the facility.

JENNA, mother to Cassie and Deirdre

"As a single mother, I constantly struggled with how to handle public bathrooms. I have the bladder of a camel, so I can be out in public for an entire day without going to the bathroom. I quickly learned my kids are not capable of the same feat. Unfortunately for them and me, I have an extreme fear of germs. I decided ahead of time that I would simply cover the seat if they had to use the bathroom. When the time came to let my daughters use the bathroom, however, I realized nobody can move that fast. When they said they needed to go, they needed to GO! I wanted at least two, if not three or four, layers of toilet paper on the seat before they sat down, but my younger daughter wet her pants the first time I tried that! She learned from that experience to tell me a little bit sooner, and I learned that one layer of paper would have to suffice. Since then, we've done much better about using public bathrooms and just last week we began leaving the house without a diaper! We are still learning, but at least now I know it's something we have to learn together."

Reverting to a Diaper

As you come to terms with when and how to use a public restroom, many parents struggle with knowing when it is necessary to revert to a diaper or pull-up. This question often comes into play when a family has a long road trip, plane flight, or serious, lengthy situation (such as a death in the family) where potty training may not be able to take precedence or bathrooms may simply not be available with the frequency that potty training requires. When these situations present themselves, many parents turn back to diapers to help them prevent accidents that would otherwise require a change of clothes and more than one potentially embarrassing scenario. While diapers are a safe way to prevent your child from soiling her clothes while alleviating bathroom responsibilities in what are already difficult situations, there are many drawbacks to consider.

First, your child knows what a diaper means as much as you do. Therefore, if you have your child wear and use a diaper in lieu of a bathroom, you may be encouraging regression. She is more likely to become comfortable again with having urine or feces in her pants, just as she is more likely to let go of the embarrassment of relieving herself in her pants. If you choose to use the diaper for more than a short period of time, you are also relieving her of the responsibility of listening to her body on when she needs to go to the bathroom. When you take the diaper off and revert to underwear, you may find that she is not mature enough or old enough to realize it is once again her responsibility to pay attention to signs and find an appropriate bathroom facility.

Another potential problem comes in the form of discomfort for your child. At this point, she is familiar with using a bathroom and enjoying clean, dry pants throughout the day. For some children there can be psychological ramifications for being encouraged to once again soil a diaper. She may feel that it is dirty and actually end up holding her urine for an unsafe amount of time to save herself the shame of being dirty or of "being a baby." You may think you are doing the child a favor by giving her an easy outlet to relieve herself, when in fact you might just be causing her shame and physical pain.

It is important to consider your child's particularities before even thinking about reverting back to a diaper for a short period of time. Is your child pretty easing going? Does she adapt well to changes? If so she may do just fine with a brief reversion to a diaper. If you child shows any rigidity with change, you may want to reconsider reverting back to the diaper. It could easily send a message that is conflicting and disturbing to your child. It is best to only move forward and never take steps backward with children who tend to have a harder time with change.

Don't be afraid to put your child's needs first when it comes to potty training. It is a brief but important time in their lives and an equally important milestone in your parenting career. You will find that most facilities and their employees will be sympathetic to your child's needs. Of course you will find some individuals who are not particularly helpful, and it is important in those moments for you to stay calm. In all likelihood your child will be in distress and your agitation will only exacerbate the problem. Only ask to see the manager quickly if there is time; if there isn't time you can consider looking the employee squarely in the eye and calmly explaining that a failure to provide a restroom immediately will result in a public health emergency that he or she will be forced to clean up. That has a tendency to open an available restroom. Mothers of boys can usually recount at least one episode of their sons urinating in a disposable bottle during a long car trip. Boys tend to find this a great novelty, so it should only be used in extreme situations. Of course, for girls it is not even an option. However, if are going on a camping trip or long car ride with no hope of finding restrooms, you might want to consider investing in portable urinals. They even make a female version.

The main thing is to have a problem-solving mentality about your travels. You know your child is going to need to use a bathroom. Plan accordingly and be prepared for emergencies with extra wipes, and a change of clothes. Remember to keep your sense of humor.

What a Child Should Know as Potty Training Ends

Children are miraculous creatures; they love to learn new and exciting things. Potty training is just another adventure to them, one filled with new behaviors, words, places, and feelings. At the end of potty training, a child should have a basic understanding of how his body functions and what it feels like when the urge to use a bathroom nears. For some children, the knowledge and the urge may happen at the instant that finding a toilet becomes an immediate necessity. Don't worry; with your helpful reminders you will see his ability to recognize the urge and still have time to make it to the bathroom grow.

Children also need to have a basic understanding of how bathroom fixtures work. They may not be able to flush the toilet by themselves, but they should understand the necessity of flushing after using the toilet. Likewise, they need to understand how a faucet works, and that the water must be turned on and then off. The turning on part is usually infinitely more interesting to them, but the turning off part will save your water bill, your bathroom floor, and the environment! Knowing how the fixtures work goes hand in hand with knowledge of bathroom etiquette. You will want to instill the values that are appropriate for your home environment, but there are some basics that all children should be taught about hygiene and manners surrounding the bathroom. Obviously there is flushing and washing of hands, but there are also conventions concerning closing the door, knocking when the door is closed, and checking to make sure your child is fully clothed before exiting the bathroom. These are all important steps for the potty-trained children to know.

Hygiene is, of course, one of the biggest areas of concern. Taking the time during potty training to teach children to properly wipe, to dispose of used tissue, and to always wash their hands with soap and water is key to any potty-training regimen. Now that your child is using the bathroom, remember to praise not only the entire skill set, and that includes his hands properly.

Last but not least, children should know that accidents happen to everyone. Many children will try to hide accidents for fear of recrimination, so encourage him to be honest with you even if he has an accident. Giving your child a sense of self-esteem about his accomplishments to go with the knowledge that you are on his side no matter what will lay a strong foundation for all of the challenges he will face after potty training.

 **Essential**

> It may seem like a tall order, but if these steps are included in potty training, they make the transition out of potty training that much easier. Boys who are taught that putting the toilet seat down is part of going to the bathroom don't have to be retaught these types of basic courtesies at the age of fourteen or twenty-seven.

What a Parent Should Know as Potty Training Ends

There is no doubt that you have heard this before: accidents happen, and, boy do they! You must be ready to manage accidents at home as well as away from home. Take an extra change of clothes for your child with you each time you leave home. Parents and children tend to become less frustrated and angry when they are prepared for an accident. Taking a change of clothes and underwear is almost as an insurance policy that nothing will happen. Have you ever noticed that when you have your umbrella it doesn't rain? The parallels are similar.

> **KIM, mother of Erin, age 6**
> "After my child potty trained and was a little older, she still had accidents from time to time. Remembering to take extra clothing, panties, and wipes was a challenge. I remedied this by keeping a change of underwear and clothing in a large Ziploc bag in my car. I also kept baby wipes in a smaller Ziploc so that a quick trip to the parking lot could solve our problem."

Doing a Big Job in a Different Potty

A common issue seen in children is the avoidance of having a bowel movement in any setting other than their own home (and many grownups have this same challenge). As previously discussed, stool withholding is a dangerous habit to form. It creates a cycle of holding followed by constipation that results in painful bowel movements. If this cycle continues, your child may have further problems with constipation, leading to urinary accidents. If you notice this pattern taking shape, encourage your child to use the potty as soon as she feels the urge. Discuss your concerns with her teachers so that they may gently encourage her as well. Helping your child understand that peeing and pooping are natural parts of life (everyone does it) is a great way to promote good potty habits.

Even the most brilliant child will occasionally have an accident, sometimes even years after potty training has completed. Be patient. Be prepared. Take these accidents in stride. Losing your temper will not help anyone. Instead, think like a scientist and ask yourself, "What were the circumstances that lead to this accident?" Is there a way you can help your child to avoid another accident? Do you need to remind her more often to use the restroom at regular intervals? Do you need to limit fluids before bedtime?

One word of caution: don't ignore potty-training accidents, especially if they recur. Sometimes children will begin having accidents as a symptom of something else that is bothering them. It is not unusual for children to have accidents after a death in the family, at the start of school, during a divorce, or with some other trauma. If the source of your child's anxiety is not readily apparent, do some sleuthing and get to the bottom of it. Any significant regression in potty training should warrant a trip to the pediatrician.

Continue to Remind Your Child

It is important after potty training is completed to remind your child at regular intervals to use the bathroom. He is now busy with other things, making friends and navigating his way through a world of new things, so he is not always going to remember to use the bathroom. Your job is still to remind him and praise him when he uses the bathroom successfully. Build self-esteem by reminding him that you are proud of him, that he is a big boy and is doing a great job! Remind him of all the steps after using the potty: flushing, pulling up his pants, and washing his hands. Keep the praise coming; you are anchoring for him that he is capable of doing great things all on his own.

Watch for the Potty Dance

You'll notice that when you child is engrossed in a preferred activity, her brain will stay focused on what she is doing while her body will start telegraphing that it is time to go to the bathroom. The famous potty dance lets you know that it is time to be the voice of her body talking to her brain. You build a stronger connection between her brain and her body each time you see the potty dance and verbally remind your child to use the restroom. Soon she will recognize the symptoms herself, even during her favorite activities, but for now, and for quite a while to come, you will need to continue to reinforce this connection.

Transitioning from a Child's Potty to a Toilet

At some point you will want to make the transition from the potty chair to the toilet. Generally it is a good idea to give this transition a great deal of lead up time. If you feel it would help, you may want to pair it with a non–person-related milestone, like a birthday. A month before the birthday you can begin by talking about how old he is going to be and all the big boy things that come with that birthday. Include going to the bathroom on the big boy potty like Mommy and Daddy on the list of things that a big boy can do. If your child is excited and expresses an interest in being on the big boy potty, let him! Praise him for a job well done. If he expresses fear about the potty, don't force the issue but do continue to talk about what a big boy he will be when he does try the big boy potty. Try to pair positive things that he wants to do with the big-boy potty. Does he want to play on your computer? That is something big boys do, so if he wants to be a big boy and play on a computer he has to use the big-boy potty. Give him time to adjust to the idea, but don't force it. Once he does use the toilet, make a praise party and be sure to reinforce the behavior with other big boy things, maybe even a present!

It is a good idea to fade the potty chair out slowly and not draw too much attention to it. Potty training was fun and some good times were had on that potty chair, so you may find that your growing child is a little attached to the chair. Try moving the chair slowly out of the bathroom, a little every day. If your child doesn't seem to notice, try putting the chair in a closet for a week, then the garage, and ultimately completely out of the house (as in the garbage) or in a box if you are planning on having more kids. Do not be surprised when, even years from now, your child sees that chair and reacts like he has been reunited with a long lost friend. This reaction is still better than having him cringe and run in fear.

Closing Thoughts

Potty training is one of the most important developmental tasks your child will tackle during toddlerhood. It can be a simple one for some, while others struggle with each aspect of training. No two children will potty train exactly the same. In a family with four children, it is likely that parents will use four different methods to help each child accomplish the goal. No matter the method used, ultimately each child will be successful at mastering the task.

Parental support and encouragement of your child is necessary throughout the potty-training process. Toddlers are working toward developing autonomy and independence during this time. Children absorb every bit of input from their environments—positive and negative. In order to develop a strong, healthy self-image, the majority of the input must be positive. If negative input, such as scolding and punishment for accidents, is received, the child learns to be ashamed and doubts her abilities. Therefore, negative reinforcement must be avoided during this critical time period. Providing positive, consistent reactions ensures that each toddler moves into early childhood with a sense of well-being.

If you have not done so already, enlist the experience of parents with children around your child's same age to gain insight into the potty-training process. You may be pleasantly surprised with the suggestions made. As with all advice, use the pearls that are appropriate and comfortable for you and your family. Avoid listening to those who regale you with their heroic tales of potty training a child (usually the child was your spouse and the tall tale tellers are your in-laws) at the age of twelve months. You have learned that this is developmentally inappropriate. Potty training before age two is less about a child's ability and more about the parent's discipline.

Determining your child's readiness for potty training is the single most important step in the process. Beginning training before a child is really ready only creates frustration and extends the amount of time the process takes to complete. There is an increasing amount of information that points out a link between training a child too early and increased accidents later. It is thought that this is related to the stress and anxiety of the child during the potty-training period. For this reason, it is recommended that potty training begin according to your child's developmental age instead of her chronological age.

Once the potty-training process has begun, consistency, as always, is key because children love and require routine. It is necessary, therefore, to discuss potty training with each caregiver, parent, family member, and teacher that will be around your child during the potty-training process. It is important that each person in her life uses the same words, methods, and encouragement as your child works on staying dry. Providing this consistent routine is one more way to ensure her successful transition to the next developmental stage.

Now, having made it a point to discuss consistency, it is equally important to realize when you must stop the process and regroup. Often parents assess readiness in their children and allow for minor deficits in their development. For example, they'll make an excuse for the occasional waking with wet diapers after a nap. If too many of these allowances are made, they add up to a child who is not developmentally ready to begin, but because the parent was ready, the process was begun anyway. If you have begun the potty-training process but have become frustrated due to the frequent challenges or accidents, it is okay to stop the process and wait for a little while longer. Remember, your goal is to help your child successfully transition into independence. If you are frustrated or angry most of the time over her struggles with using the potty, your child is likely to develop anxiety and fears that prohibit her from feeling autonomous.

This book is meant to serve as a guide for potty training. Hopefully you have gleaned helpful information specific to your needs from its pages. Use the experience of others to help you. Your health care provider is an excellent source of information, so talk to her about potty training. She may have other pearls of wisdom that will help you. Although this guide has taken a comprehensive approach, it is likely there are pieces of information that have not been included or were only briefly mentioned. To assist you in further reading about your chosen method, resources have been provided in the appendices to help you in your journey as you and your toddler successfully achieve a diaper-free life.

Good luck!

Frequently Asked Questions

The following questions cover the basic concepts of what parents typically ask as they begin potty training, experience problems along the way, or find themselves with long-term concerns regarding their child's progress. For more in-depth answers, each question relates to one or more earlier chapters.

How will I know when my child is ready to begin potty training?

In order to even consider potty training, you as the parent have to understand that every child is different in all aspects of life, and this includes potty training. There is no one age or developmental stage that marks a readiness for potty training in every single child. While girls do typically learn potty training at an earlier age than boys, this is still a pattern and not a rule. In order to determine if your child is ready to begin potty training, you can consult the questions in the preceding chapters that focus on following commands, physically being able to handle clothing, and demonstrating general awareness of the body and its functions.

My child is under the age of two but sometimes seems interested in potty training. Should I begin the process even though he is under the recommended age?

Although some guides will offer recommended ages, a calendar age is nothing more than a record of how many days, weeks, and months your child has been alive. You should begin potty training your child whenever he shows general readiness for it. If you are worried that he may be too young to retain what you teach him, find a slower method works best for you. If you begin potty training and realize as you progress that your child is not ready after all, that is okay. You can stop the process at one point and pick it up again later, and you and your child will still benefit from the lessons you have already taught him.

Is there a better time in life to begin potty training than others?

Once you have established that your child is ready, you also need to make sure you are ready. If you have highly turbulent times in your future, including travel, divorce, or moving, you may find that it is best to wait to potty train. Once you are sure you are in a good place in your life station to begin potty training, you also need to consider which method you will use. If you want to pursue a boot camp method that focuses on intensive sessions packed into one or two days, you need to have two days when you will be able to stay home and focus on nothing else. If you are looking at a slower approach, such as the Brazelton method, your day-to-day schedule will represent less interference with your child's potty training.

What is the best method to use for potty training?

Like the age when your child begins potty training, the method that will serve you best depends greatly on your child and your own parenting methods. You will need to carefully consider the amount of time you wish to invest in this process, the speed at which your child typically learns and then practices new behaviors, and whether you wish to use praise, rewards, or directives in order to potty train your child. Once you have established your preferences for all of these factors, you will be able to see which method will work best for you and your family.

Do we have to use a potty chair?

The short answer is no, you do not have to use a potty chair. Whether you choose to use a potty chair or a potty seat that fits on your own toilet should be based on your house and your child. If you do choose to use a potty chair, you need to consider where you will keep it and how long you will use it. It is usually best to keep a potty chair in the bathroom near the regular toilet for sanitary reasons and to avoid confusion later on when your child learns to use the regular toilet. If you choose not to use a potty chair, you will need to make sure you have a stepping stool that allows your child to reach the toilet on her own and then plant her feet for better positioning when she has a bowel movement.

My child is very fidgety when he sits on the potty. What can I do to help him sit still and how important is this?

In the beginning, it is normal for your child to be fidgety on the potty. You will have to put him on the potty more often than he will need to go, and you may need to have him sit for extended periods of time (five to ten minutes as opposed to one to two minutes). However, fidgeting can make it harder for his bladder and bowels to relax. In order to help him, you need to focus on overcoming any fears he may have about the toilet and while also making the toilet an enjoyable place to be. Some parents bring toys into the bathroom to make their children less fidgety, but this solution again raises questions of cleanliness (particularly for little boys who are still learning how to direct their spray). You can also use songs, conversation, and small games to help keep your child entertained while you wait for him to eliminate.

Is there an advantage to using diapers rather than training pants during potty training?

Training pants are typically more expensive than diapers, but they do have their advantages. First, although the overall package of training pants is more expensive than the same number of diapers, training pants can be worn as long as it stays dry. Diapers are more likely to rip and the adhesive is less likely to last, making it necessary to use a new diaper every time your child tries to go to the bathroom. Similarly, training pants also make your child more involved in dressing and undressing herself when she goes to the potty and they are more like the process she will follow once she switches to big girl underwear.

When should I stop using diapers? When should I stop using training pants?

As soon as you have started actively potty training your child (i.e., moved past early discussions and into sitting on the potty), you should consider switching to training pants. Remember that the final goal is not just a diaper-free child, but an independent, diaper-free child. For this reason, your child needs to be able to dress and undress himself. Once you have experienced two consecutive dry days, you can consider switching out of training pants and into underwear. This does not mean that you will now be accident-free, but your child needs to experience the rewards of becoming a big boy as he achieves them, so you do not want to wait too long before you let him change out of the training pants.

My daughter insists on wiping back to front rather than front to back. What should I do?

This is a problem that spans generations. Wiping back to front results in pulling bacteria into your daughter's vagina, which can then lead to yeast infections, urinary tract infections, and more. If your daughter has already had an infection as a result of wiping back to front, you can remind her of this in the moment she is wiping to help her link the cause to the effect. You can also try having her stand up to wipe in the beginning. Standing will alleviate her fears of falling in to the toilet, and it may also make it easier for her to reach the necessary areas. Finally, demonstrations help. If you haven't already, now would be a good time to let your daughter go to the bathroom with you. If you have already let her come with you, keep doing so, but now make sure you are talking to her as you demonstrate how to wipe. This does not need to be an invasive display for you or your daughter. Rather, this will be a simple show where she sees the motions your hand makes when you are in the process of wiping. If none of this works, you may want to continue to wipe for her while you first master keeping her diaper dry, and then teach her the importance of proper wiping at a later time.

Is it okay to use alcohol-based cleaners rather than soap and water after my child goes to the bathroom?

Alcohol-based cleaners are very helpful in day-to-day activities, but it is necessary for you and your child to use soap and water when the cleaning involves bodily fluids. It is impossible to be absolutely certain that your hands (and your child's hands) are completely clean of bodily fluids when using the bathroom, so soap and water should be used every time. You can still use an alcohol-based cleaner after the soap and water for extra sanitation if you so desire, but it is not necessary.

What if my child stops using the potty?

Many children go through the process, become fully potty trained, and then promptly begin to regress. Children will maintain dry pants but begin relieving themselves in corners, outside, or on the floor. Some children begin having accidents all over again, while others insist on returning to a diaper for no apparent reason. The only rule here is that there is no tried-and-true rule for when your child will be regression-free. If your child stops using the potty, this just means that you need to backtrack and revisit some of your earlier potty-training lessons. If you try this and your child still refuses to use the potty, you may need to go back to diapers and wait a while before you return to potty training again.

Why does it take so much longer to teach my child to use the potty for bowel movements than it does for peeing?

Almost all children adapt to peeing in the potty before they adapt to bowel movements in the potty. While peeing is most often a continuous, fluid (literally) movement, bowel movements are different. Passing a solid substance often makes children more aware of the gaping area beneath them. This new experience induces feelings of vulnerability, unfamiliarity, and fear. Whether your child waits several days, several weeks, or even several months before he begins having bowel movements in the potty, rest assured that this is a normal part of potty training. As he becomes used to the potty and the feeling of relieving himself into what will still feel like a gaping hole, his body will relax and he will soon begin having bowel movements in the potty as well.

How do I know if my child is constipated?

Constipation in children is much like it is in adults, but language barriers often make it harder for a child to describe this unfamiliar ailment. If you believe your child may be constipated, look for the following signs: dry and/or hard stools, abdominal pain, difficulty passing a bowel movement, stiff and/or pebble-like stools, and streaks of blood around the stools. For more information on how to treat constipation, consult earlier chapters.

My child's urine has a strong odor. Does this mean she has an infection?

Although odors can be alarming, there are many possible contributions. Specific foods and drinks can cause a strong odor in a person's urine, particularly if she has consumed a large quantity of one specific product. Still, there are potentially serious causes for odor, such as infections, so it is best to contact your health care provider just to be on the safe side.

Is it okay to let my child urinate outside during potty training?

Between the large load of laundry that can result from accidents during potty training and the disruption in routine, many parents allow their children—particularly young boys—to urinate outside in the summertime. While this may seem like an easy solution to aid in potty training when the weather cooperates, the fact of the matter is that it is not sanitary and will not help your potty-training progress when you are indoors or when the weather makes outdoor urination impossible. There are also the sanitary concerns of the people around you to consider. While some parents will agree that outdoor urination is an easy solution and completely acceptable in a young toddler, nobody wants to walk in your child's urine. You will also find your son rapidly approaching an age when most people will not find outdoor urination acceptable, so it is always easier to advise against this habit from the very beginning.

What is the best method for teaching my child to use a public potty?

There are typically two types of children when it comes to using public restrooms. The first kind is very enthusiastic about this new and fascinating area of a store or restaurant. For these children, your task is not how to get them to use a public restroom but how to get them to wait long enough for you to make sure the toilet has the appropriate sanitation cover. For these children, act quickly and efficiently and you shouldn't have a problem.

The second type of children has a fear of public restrooms. In addition the general fear of toilets, public restrooms involve going to the bathroom around strangers, using unknown facilities, and putting yourself in a small, unfamiliar stall with the intention of "relieving" yourself. This can be nerve-racking for adults, but for children it can be downright terrifying. In order to help your child overcome this fear, you need to make her more familiar with public restrooms. Take your child into a public bathroom every time you leave the house, even if it is only to wash your hands or look in the mirror. Let your child watch you go to the bathroom in a public restroom. The more familiar you make your child with public bathrooms, the less likely she is to be afraid of the unfamiliar.

What is the best method to break my child's habit of bedwetting?

Bedwetting is a habit that continues long after children are otherwise considered potty trained. Because it can continue in children up to eight years old before there is cause for concern, you can teach certain habits to help reduce the likelihood of your child having an accident during the night. The most obvious step is to eliminate all beverages from your child's diet within two hours of going to bed. You can also try lifting, where you or your partner physically removes your child from his bed during the night and taking him to the bathroom. Bedwetting often occurs because children sleep so deeply they are unaware of their bodies' signals that they need to go to the bathroom. Lifting can disrupt a child's sleep pattern to not only give him the opportunity to go to the bathroom, but also help him realize that his body will need to wake up in the night long enough to go to the bathroom. If limiting drinks and lifting does not work, you can also try an alarm. Manufacturers of toddlers' products now make underwear lined with an alarm that will sound when dampness begins. This product has disadvantages as well as advantages, so you should read carefully about the specific details of using such underwear before making your decision. Finally, you can also consult your health care provider in order to gain more information about other options available to you to help counteract habitual bedwetting.

My child is six years old and still has nighttime accidents. Is this normal?

Whether your child just accomplished potty training in the last year or has been potty trained since she was two years old, bedwetting at this age is still very normal. In fact, bedwetting can typically occur up until a child is eight years old without causing concern. Because there are so many contributing factors to a child wetting the bed, most of which are not indicative of any medical problem, you should not worry about bedwetting as anything more than disruption in your night—and potentially day—unless your child is nine years old and still experiencing bedwetting on a regular or semi-regular basis. Remember, many habits take a long time to break. As with all other aspects of parenting, maintaining your patience with bedwetting will save you and your child considerable frustration.

Glossary

Antibacterial
obliterates or limits the existence and/or growth of bacteria

Attachment parenting
a method of parenting that typically involves near-constant contact between parent and child (e.g,. carrying an infant in a sling, co-sleeping, etc.)

Autonomy
independence, particularly when it comes to choosing a person's own actions

Bowel movement
excrement from the bowels (poop)

Candida
a yeast-like fungus present in mucous membranes in the mouth and vagina that may become pathogenic

Child-oriented
a method that focuses on the wants and needs of the child

Commode
toilet

Comorbid
two diseases that occur simultaneously

Constipation
a condition of the bowels when feces are hard and dry making it difficult to eliminate

Continuum concept parenting
similar to attachment parenting, a style of parenting that involves constant contact with parents, extended breast-feeding, and working with a child's signals to determine wants and needs starting at birth

Defecate
eliminate waste from the bowels (poop)

Elimination Communication
a potty technique that requires a parent use an infant's signals to help their child eliminate outside of a diaper as early as four months old

Encopresis
involuntary bowel movement

Enuresis
lack of urinary control; incontinence

Equilibrioception
a person's sense of balance

Gastrocolic reflex
the occurrence of peristalsis following the entrance of food into an empty stomach; responsible for the urge to defecate following a meal

Hygiene
a situation or habit contributing to the preservation of health

Hypotonia
a condition in which there is loss of muscle tone that results in stretching muscles beyond their expected limits

Interoception
sensitivity to stimuli originating outside of the body

Labia
any of the folds of skin surrounding the vulva

Magnetoception
(also known as magnetoreception) an ability to detect a magnetic field

Nociception
(also known as nocireception) an ability to perceive injurious stimuli

Parent-oriented
a method that focuses on the wants/needs of the parent

Perineal
the area in front of the anus that extends to the vulva in the female and the scrotum in the male

Phimosis
a condition in which the foreskin of the penis cannot be fully retracted

Probiotics
a beneficial bacteria

Proprioception
the sense of what your muscles and joints are doing and, related to this, where you are in space

Regression
the act of reverting to a previous condition

Smearing
in potty training, specifically refers to a toddler smearing feces around a room

Thermoception
the perception of temperature

Urinary tract infection (UTI)
a bacterial infection in the kidneys, ureters, bladder, and/or urethra

Urinate
to discharge urine (to pee)

Valsalva response
(also known as the Valsalva maneuver) a technique used by a person trying to forcibly exhale air from their body while maintaining a closed windpipe (in potty training, as it pertains to bowel movements)

Vasopressin
a peptide hormone that serves to help regulate the body's water retention

Tracking Your Child's Progress in Potty Training

Using a chart can be very helpful when monitoring your child's progress. Each section of the chart serves its own purpose toward achieving your overall goal of a diaper-free child. The date will help you monitor step-by-step progress as your child uses the toilet more and diapers less. Additionally, the date will provide you with a written record of when you began potty training. Because parents often realize they have tried to begin potty training before their children are ready, the date can help you remember how old your child was when you started and how long you should wait before you try again.

Next, the "Day in Progress" section can help you monitor how long it is taking to achieve complete potty training. If your child appears to be diaper-free after only a day or two of potty training, you have extra cause to celebrate! At the same time, you also have extra cause to watch carefully for accidents or steps toward regression. If your child is taking longer to potty train, you may want to consider taking a break from the process. Overall, monitoring the number of days in your child's potty-training progress will help you as the parent to maintain patience and rationality in what you expect of your toddler.

Finally, the time chart can help you notice patterns in your child's elimination habits, assist you in creating patterns to help your child know when to use the bathroom, and aid you both in anticipating when you will need to take your child to use the toilet. By recording the time your child uses or tries to use the toilet each day, you will be able to help yourself set up a routine for when to use the bathroom. By including diaper changes, you will also be able to see patterns in when your child tends to soil her diaper, particularly after naps or in the late afternoon when children are most likely to be tired and/or hungry.

Of course, the charts also offer the added benefit of tracking your progress. By using the time chart each day, you and your child will have a visual reminder of how she is improving and how close she is to leading a diaper-free life!

Date:	
Day in Progress	
8 A.M.:	
9 A.M.:	
10 A.M.:	
11 A.M.:	
12 P.M.:	
1 P.M.:	
2 P.M.:	
3 P.M.:	
4 P.M.:	
5 P.M.:	
6 P.M.:	
7 P.M.:	
8 P.M.:	
Coding Guide:	
W =	Wet Diaper
D =	Pooped in the Diaper
P =	Peed in the Toilet/Potty Chair
BM =	Pooped in the Toilet/Potty Chair
T =	Tried to Use the Potty/Did Not Eliminate

Resources/References

General Tips

http://letsgopotty.com
www.parentingscience.com/potty-training-techniques.html
www.pottytrainingconcepts.com
www.pottytrainingsolutions.com
www.pull-ups.com
www.sinkems.com
www.timl.com/ipt

On Potty Training Aids

www.musicalpotty.com
www.peterpotty.com
www.pottypatty.com
www.pottyscotty.com
www.pottysong.com
www.pottytrainingtps.com
www.pottytrainingrewards.com
www.thepottystool.com
www.thepottytrainer.com

On Bed Wetting and Accidents

http://bedwettingstore.com
http://kidney.niddk.nih.gov/kudiseases/pubs/
bedwetting_ez/index.htm
www.mayoclinic.com/health/potty-training/CC0000

On Elimination Communication

www.diaperfreebaby.org
www.mothering.com
www.naturalbirthandbabycare.com
www.theecstore.com

On Medical Tips

www.aap.org/publiced/BR_ToiletTrain.htm
www.askdrsears.com
http://autism.healingthresholds.com
http://contemporarypediatrics.modernmedicine.com/toilettraining
www.familydoctor.org/179.xml
www.keepkidshealthy.com
www.mayoclinic.com

On the Fast Track

www.3daypottytraining.com

Index

R

S

We Have
EVERYTHING®
on Anything!

The Everything® list spans a wide range of subjects, with more than 500 titles covering 25 different categories:

Business	History	Reference
Careers	Home Improvement	Religion
Children's Storybooks	Everything Kids	Self-Help
Computers	Languages	Sports & Fitness
Cooking	Music	Travel
Crafts and Hobbies	New Age	Wedding
Education/Schools	Parenting	Writing
Games and P		
Health	Pets	

31901050189770